Praise for

Let Your Life C

"Donna Partow is a stick of dynamite for the soul that is sick and tired of being stuck in the mundane. For every woman who has ever wanted to do something significant for God, *Let Your Life Count* is a book for you. Donna not only challenges women to rise up and take their place in the kingdom, she also encourages them to allow the Lord to take their ordinary lives and make something extraordinary out of everything they do."

—JOANNA WEAVER, best-selling author of *Having a Mary Heart in a Martha World*

"Like healing salve on a wounded heart, *Let Your Life Count* will change lives. We all long to make a difference for God. Donna Partow combines vulnerability and boldness with the strong foundation of scriptural truth to help us on the journey of finding our purpose."

—ALLISON GAPPA BOTTKE, speaker and author of *God Allows U-Turns* and debut novel *A Stitch in Time*

"If you want to shine for Jesus, read *Let Your Life Count*. Donna Partow writes a road map of the life every Christian should aspire to live. Convicting and convincing…superb wisdom and communication shines through. Your personal walk with Christ won't be the same."

—WAYNE ATCHESON, Christian Writers Guild

"*Let Your Life Count* is another zinger from Donna Partow. Every chapter challenges both my thinking and my actions. Donna has something to say to everyone: the new Christian, the seasoned believer, and the still-searching. Her stories about real people, her examination of Scripture, and her practicality make *Let Your Life Count* a catalyst for growth, beyond your average devotional or study book. She seems to be able to put her finger on the next thing you should consider in your faith journey. Her excitement jumps right off the page. It's a shake-you-out-of-your-complacency book."

—NANCY KARPENSKE, contributing editor of *Christian Standard* magazine and director of women's ministry at LifeBridge Christian Church in Longmont, Colorado

LET YOUR LIFE Count

Make a Difference
Right Where
You Are

Donna Partow

WATERBROOK
PRESS

LET YOUR LIFE COUNT
PUBLISHED BY WATERBROOK PRESS
12265 Oracle Boulevard, Suite 200
Colorado Springs, Colorado 80921
A division of Random House Inc.

Details in some anecdotes and stories have been changed to protect the identities of the persons involved.

ISBN 1-57856-959-1

Published in association with the literary agency of Alive Communications Inc., 7680 Goddard Street, Suite 200, Colorado Springs, CO 80920, www.alivecommunications.com.

Library of Congress Cataloging-in-Publication Data
Partow, Donna.
    Let your life count : make a difference right where you are / Donna Partow.
       p. cm.
    Includes bibliographical references.
    ISBN 1-57856-959-1
    1. Christian women—Religious life. 2. Spiritual life—Christianity. I. Title.
    BV4527.P374 2006
    248.4—dc22

                                                        2006008618

Printed in the United States of America
2006—First Edition

10 9 8 7 6 5 4 3 2 1

CONTENTS

A NOTE FROM DONNA

*F*or more than a decade I've listened (in person, online, and over the airwaves) to the heartbeats of today's Christian women from around the world. What I'm hearing is this: we want our lives to count. We want to know that we can make a difference—in small ways and large—in our homes, in our communities, and on the planet. In my travels I've met women living in inner cities, in the suburbs, and in remote jungle villages who have yielded their daily routines to God...with powerful and meaningful results.

You will meet some of these women in the pages of this book, but it is my prayer that we can come together in a more personal way via online community. As you read this book, I hope you'll join us to share *your story* and *your insights*. I envision an ever-expanding network of individuals, small groups, churches, and organizations banding together to "spur one another on toward love and good deeds" (Hebrews 10:24). If you'd like to be part of this community, please visit us at www.donnapartow.com.

To help you work through this material in a small group setting, I've created a Let Your Life Count Leader's Forum (www.donnapartow .com/lylc_leaders) complete with a teacher's manual, downloadable handouts, ready-to-use PowerPoint presentations, free audios, links to resources, and much more. If your church would like to sponsor a Let Your Life Count conference, please e-mail lylc@donnapartow.com.

There's no greater joy, no more-certain source of confidence, than knowing the God of the universe is carrying out His grand plan through you. In this book you'll find practical steps you can take to make yourself more available to Him and increasingly aware of His work around you. But one of the most important steps you can take is to make the decision not to journey alone. Won't you join us?

I have raised you up for this very purpose, that I
might show you my power and that my name might
be proclaimed in all the earth.

EXODUS 9:16

1

Your Life Can Count

Then the righteous will answer him, "Lord, when did we see you hungry and feed you, or thirsty and give you something to drink? When did we see you a stranger and invite you in, or needing clothes and clothe you? When did we see you sick or in prison and go to visit you?"

The King will reply, "I tell you the truth, whatever you did for one of the least of these brothers of mine, you did for me."

MATTHEW 25:37–40

Few people will ever forget the day Hurricane Katrina ripped through the Gulf Coast, doing billions of dollars' worth of damage and driving tens of thousands of people from their homes.[1] It was a disaster of mind-boggling proportions that mobilized some people and immobilized others. Many looked at the magnitude of the task and decided there was no point in getting involved. *What can one person do?* they said to themselves. Others rolled up their sleeves and did what they could.

This was the case with one pastor I heard interviewed on Christian radio.[2] He said that as his congregation gathered on Sunday morning, they noticed a traffic jam forming on the nearby freeway as people fled the coastal areas. As the realization dawned, they decided to serve rather than continue with the service. They went to the freeway and beckoned travelers to the church where the travelers received food, shelter, and comfort. At midnight, as the building overflowed with nearly two thousand harried hurricane victims, the pastor called a nearby church and explained that people were still flooding in. That church, too, soon became a sanctuary from one of the worst natural disasters in American history.

But we don't have to be on the outskirts of a hurricane or some other disaster to let our lives count. We can reach out to the people who cross our paths each day; all we have to do is let God work through us. People are fleeing personal disasters every hour of every day, on every freeway and byway in America, not to mention every dirt road in every nation on earth. No doubt at least one of these—Hurricane Divorce, Hurricane Cancer, and Hurricane Unemployment, just to name three—struck in your neighborhood today. Hurricane AIDS is decimating the continent of Africa while Hurricane Terrorism wreaks havoc throughout the Middle East and even Europe.

Please don't think this is a book about Christian activism, although in some ways it is. It's really about living the way we were intended: loving God and caring about people (see Matthew 22:36–40). I used to believe only big gestures counted in the grand scheme of things. I was wrong. The hope and healing we offer as we wipe away the tears of a friend or lighten the load of a stranger have just as much value.

We're coming to the end of another hot summer here in Phoenix, where it's been up to 117 degrees. Last week, as my daughter and I were driving home from the pharmacy, I noticed that a public bus had broken down. The driver and two stranded passengers were sitting nearby, frying in the three-digit temperature. I know they say it's a dry heat, but trust me, it's absolutely unbearable when it's that hot, dry or not! As I drove past that broken-down bus, my heart broke for those people.

My mind flashed back to the time in my life when I stood on sweltering, overcrowded buses, commuting in and out of the West Philadelphia neighborhood where I lived, getting by on thirteen dollars a week for groceries. So I turned my air-conditioned car around and offered to be their bus for the day. They were overjoyed by the small act of kindness. I let them know we helped them because God had prompted us to, and I mentioned the church we attend. I pray it counted for the kingdom; I know it lifted my spirits to spend a few minutes thinking about someone other than me, myself, and I.

This is not the book I was hired to write, but I'm writing it anyway and I want to tell you why. Within the last month, my teenage nephew died—suddenly and tragically—and my father suffered congestive heart failure. He is now dying, slowly and inevitably. I've been reflecting not only on their lives but also on my own. More than anything, I want to know that when I'm gone it will have mattered that I walked the planet. I want to know that my life counted for something, not just to readers or audience members (though I'm profoundly thankful for all of you!), but to people around me—you know, people who might actually show up at my funeral. Will those people who watched my life up close and personal say I pointed them to God just by the way I conducted myself each day?

I had been struggling with the infamous writer's block (which I always thought was pure fiction, but I now know is only too real) for more than a year when these two events unfolded. One day, the thought came to me: *If I could write only one more book, what would it be? What would I say if I knew my days were numbered (which, of course, they are—see Psalm 139:16)?* The words leaped out of my mouth: "Let your life count." I would stand on the highest mountain and shout, "Let your life count!"

After more than two decades of following Jesus, I've discovered that:

- Who we are speaks louder than what we say.
- Who we are accomplishes more than anything we could
  ever do.

That's why one of my recent books was entitled *Becoming the Woman I Want to Be.* Being must precede doing. God created us as human *beings,* not human *doings.* However, God's first order of business was to give people work to do. He put Adam in the garden and told him to get busy naming animals and tending the earth. God desires for us to lead fruitful lives in which who we are is manifested in what we do, in which what we believe transforms the way we live.

My message is this: when who we are and how we live reflect God's heart, our lives will truly count for eternity.

Nothing else matters! A life lived for yourself is empty, no matter how rich you are. And a life lived for God and others is rich, no matter how empty your wallet. It's not about us, and it's not about stuff—it's about Him, His kingdom, and introducing people to His kingdom.

I firmly believe that our lives can and will count, in small ways and large, in ways we might expect and in ways beyond our imaginations, if we'll simply open our eyes to the world around us and open our hearts to the possibility that we might be the answer to someone's prayer. Since you've picked up a book entitled *Let Your Life Count*, I know you believe that as well. My goal is to inspire and motivate you to move forward in faith, to take a few steps—some baby steps, some big steps—in obedience to God's call. You don't have to be anyone other than who you are, and, unless God tells you otherwise, it's probably best to start right where you are. If I could convince you of one thing, it would be this: God is working everywhere, even in your neighborhood, and especially in your heart.

Please don't take this journey alone! Share the experience with women around the world in our online Let Your Life Count Community. Let us encourage and challenge you, even as you share your insights and experiences with others. Visit www.donnapartow.com/lylc_community for details. If you'd like to share this material with a group in your community, visit www.donnapartow.com/lylc_leaders for a free Leader's Manual, downloadable handouts, ready-to-use Power Point presentations, free audios, links to resources, and much more.

Maybe you're thinking, *That sounds great in theory, but exactly how is this book going to help me?* Will this book show me, step by step, the pathway to letting my life count? Well, that's my goal! When you turn to the next chapter, you'll find out why it's okay to "Just Be Yourself" and be reassured that letting your life count doesn't have to be an emotionally exhausting ordeal. It won't be when you "Don't Try to Make Your Life Count." Instead, you'll be blessed to "Discover God-Directed Prayer" and find practical suggestions to help you "Live Daily in God's Presence." As you begin to *listen* in prayer and walk with an awareness of God throughout the day, you'll discover that "You Were Created to Be a Sign That God Cares" and, in fact, "God Has Prepared Good Works for You to Do."

Too often when we think about serving God, we immediately think of serving at church, and we worry that we're not as spiritual, qualified, or well-informed as everyone else sitting in the pews around us. However, "You Don't Have to Be a Church Insider to Count." A wide variety of opportunities exists to let your life count, and few of them require a theological degree. Even so, maybe you feel inadequate. You're not alone, so "Don't Wait Until You Feel Good Enough" to get involved or you'll end up waiting a long time! I hope to convince you that you're as good as everybody else but that, at the same time, it's important for all of us to "Walk in Humility."

An important component of letting your life count is keeping your motives in check. That's why I share from my own life journey some of the wrong motives that have hindered my effectiveness. The only legitimate and lasting motive for service is to "Let Christ's Love

Compel You" rather than to be compelled by duty or a selfish desire to get something in return. Only Christ's compelling love can provide the strength it takes to "Press Through Hindrances" and can empower you to "Dare to Do the Thing You Dread." We all have fears and personal insecurities; we all face challenges and difficulties. But that doesn't mean our lives can't count. Instead, you'll find it's possible to "Do It Afraid," knowing that anything can count, yes, "Even Your Problems Can Count," although you must "Be Willing to Sacrifice."

I hope to encourage you to believe that you truly can "Let Every Season Count" and that your opportunities are not restricted by age or anything else, as long as you "Maintain a Teachable Heart." In fact, "Even When You Fall, God Can Still Use You" as long as you "Develop a Marathon Mentality," knowing that sometimes you'll run, sometimes you'll crawl, but God Himself is the One who has promised to get you across that finish line.

Each chapter concludes with three components: Remember, Reflect, and Reach. "Remember" recaps the central point of each chapter. These, along with a key related scripture verse, are included in the back of the book for easy reference. "Reflect" features questions for deeper reflection that can be used personally and to facilitate group discussions. "Reach" suggests a practical next step you can take that will enable you to let your life count, right now, right where you are. These are steps you can take on your own or in conjunction with others.

To get the most out of this book, you should prayerfully consider working through it with others who share your desire to let your life count. Don't be a reader; be an implementer! Perhaps set a goal to step out of your comfort zone at least once a week and apply what you are learning. The best way to ensure faithful follow-through is to establish accountability, even if just one person will routinely ask you, "How did you let your life count this week?"

My prayer for you is that this book will represent a new chapter in your life, a new season of both accepting where you are *and* believing God wants to take you to new places—in your relationship with Him, in your community, and maybe even around the world. Your life can count!

Remember

Your life can and will count, in small ways and large, in ways you might expect and in ways beyond your imagination, if you'll simply open your eyes to the world around you and open your heart to the possibility that you might be someone's answer to prayer.

Reflect

Do you sense that your life counts? Do you sincerely believe your life can count, right where you are? Why or why not? What do you think is standing between you and the life you truly want to live? What do you hope to gain by working through this book?

Contact several people who might want to take this journey alongside you. If you are part of a small group or Sunday-school class, propose this for the next study. At a minimum, identify one person who will encourage you to let your life count and hold you accountable to finish what you've started.

Dear heavenly Father, I thank You for reassuring me today that my life can and will count. In the coming days and weeks, I invite You to speak to my heart to encourage me as I realize the ways my life already counts and to challenge me to stretch in new areas. I believe my life can count, in small ways and large, as I open my heart and make myself available to You. Lord, I want to be the answer to someone's prayer today. Maybe even inviting others to join me in this journey will be an answer, not only to my prayer, but to their prayers as well. Lead me to the person (or people) who can both encourage and challenge me. Amen.

2

Just Be Yourself

For by the grace given me I say to every one of you: Do not think of yourself more highly than you ought, but rather think of yourself with sober judgment, in accordance with the measure of faith God has given you. Just as each of us has one body with many members, and these members do not all have the same function, so in Christ we who are many form one body, and each member belongs to all the others. We have different gifts, according to the grace given us.

ROMANS 12:3–6

I'll never forget the day I spoke at a conference alongside Patsy Clairmont. Here's how the schedule went: she spoke, I spoke, she spoke, everyone forgot I spoke. At that point in my not exactly illustrious career, I could easily count the number of messages I'd delivered. However, I had purchased one of Patsy's tapes from Focus on the Family because a speech coach had told me she was the best in the business. I listened to that tape over and over again until I could have *delivered* Patsy's message for her. I really, really wanted to be Patsy

Clairmont. Patsy, being a very sharp lady, figured that out simply by listening to me as I tried to be her—and she graciously encouraged me to develop my own style.

So I looked for someone else I could become just like. I even took a training class that instructed me on how to drape myself in scarves (scarves used to be *quite the thing*)! I purchased several and made a valiant attempt to appear refined, but I never did get the knack for it. Instead, the scarves kept falling off my shoulders, and I looked like a nut (which, of course, is only appropriate). After much prayer and contemplation, I decided that I really, really, really wanted to be one of Billy Graham's daughters. If I live to be one hundred years old, I'll never forget the day I heard a Voice from heaven say, *You're not Billy Graham's daughter; get over it.* Okay, so the Voice wasn't audible, but I knew it was God nonetheless.

Although I understood that being grafted into the First Family of Christendom was out of the question, I wasn't ready to give up the quest to become someone other than me. In recent years, I've driven my family and friends crazy trying to follow in the footsteps of yet *another* famous Christian Bible teacher who shall remain nameless. Amazingly enough, God hasn't blessed any of my attempts to become someone I'm not. Do you think maybe that's because He wants me to just be myself? Nah! That can't be it!

In Acts 8, we encounter someone else who was trying to become someone he was never intended to be. His name was Simon the Sorcerer. Simon amazed the people of Jerusalem by performing magic tricks. Then he became a Christian and was baptized. The Bible doesn't question the authenticity of Simon's conversion, but it does tell us he

quickly shipwrecked his newfound faith. How? By trying to be someone he wasn't. Notice how harmlessly it all begins: "And he followed
Philip everywhere, astonished by the great signs and miracles he saw"
(verse 13). Unfortunately, Simon wasn't following Philip to learn and
grow as a disciple; he wanted to become Philip; he wanted to become
an apostle.

Isn't that how it starts for us, as well? We see someone—at work,
at church, on television. Or we read about a woman in a magazine or
a book. And we are so amazed by the great things she can do! *Wow,
that woman can bring home the bacon and fry it up in the pan! What a
spiritual giant! What an awesome ministry!* Admiration is wonderful.
Asking that person to mentor us might prove even more wonderful.
But when we react by coveting her talents, opportunities, or lifestyle,
our very own shipwreck is on the horizon. That was certainly the case
with Simon.

He didn't think his life counted anymore because he no longer
had large crowds following him. It's unfortunate that even as Christians we often measure our lives by how much applause we get and
our accomplishments by how much attention they draw. In truth,
God is far more interested in who we are when no one's watching and

If you need help discovering who you are, take the Skills
and Interests Inventory. Visit www.donnapartow.com/
lylc_inventory.

in what we do when we will get nothing in return. Eventually, Simon's attempts to be someone "important" landed him in big trouble. Some time later, when Peter and John came to Jerusalem and began dispensing the gift of the Holy Spirit through the laying on of hands, Simon offered them money if they would give him the same ability. Peter rebuked him, saying, "You have no part or share in this ministry, because your heart is not right before God" (verse 21). In particular, Peter pointed out that Simon was "full of bitterness" (verse 23).

When we compare our lives—especially our positions, gifts, and opportunities—to someone who has more than we have, we set ourselves up to become full of bitterness too. Simon wasn't content with the knowledge that he had been saved by grace and baptized into the family of God. It wasn't enough that he enjoyed the privilege of listening to Philip's teaching; it wasn't enough that he could witness the power of God at work through the apostles. No, he couldn't enjoy where God had placed him because he wanted to be someone he was not.

How about you? I sincerely hope you do not waste your valuable time and energy trying to be someone you're not. Are you a stay-at-home mom trying to keep up with the lifestyles enjoyed by two-income families? Or are you a working mother trying to compete with the homemaking accomplishments of a stay-at-home mom? Are you a servant trying to be a teacher or a prophet trying to exercise gifts of mercy? The Bible says we have different gifts and different calls (Romans 12:3–8 and 1 Corinthians 12:4–30). God wants His church to accomplish a wide variety of missions, and accomplishing these tasks will require a wide variety of people. When we try to be someone we're not, we are not only robbing ourselves of contentment, but we're also robbing the world of everything God wants to do through *us*.

My friend Deanna worked for several years as a housecleaner. As a result, she was by herself and rarely saw another person all day long. But she would sometimes pray, *Lord, let me make a difference in at least one person's life today.* Inevitably, after praying, she would either run into someone she knew or a complete stranger who needed something. She responded to those opportunities by helping however she could.

Here is one small example. One of the homeowners unexpectedly showed up in the middle of the day and was having a problem with his cell phone. Deanna recalls, "He was very stressed because he was busy running his own business and needed his phone 24/7! He thought he would have to take time to go to the cell phone store. I picked up the phone, hit a few buttons, and voilà! All I had to do was turn the ringer back on. He was so grateful! I don't think I ever saw that man again, and I cleaned his house for almost a year. But I felt like God used me to de-stress his life a bit."

Deanna adds, "The truth is, cleaning people's houses—doing a great job, showing up when I said I would, and praying for them while I clean—can make a difference in these people's lives all by itself. All of us affect someone else every day. These seem like little things that don't matter, but they matter to the other person, and they matter to God because if we've done it for someone else, we've done it for Him. He takes those things and multiplies them just like He did the loaves and fishes."

Yes, a praying housecleaner counts!

Whoever you are, whatever you do, do it all to the glory of God, and He will make it count. My fellow author Sandy Wood shared the following story[1] that beautifully illustrates how something seemingly mundane can count for the kingdom:

> Joan doesn't think of herself as a missionary. She thinks of her-
> self as the mother of eight children. Although she's no author-
> ity on evangelistic strategies, she is an expert on what children
> need most: a kind look, a soft touch, and a warm embrace.
> On her first visit to Malawi, Joan noted the ragged, tattered
> clothes worn by the orphans. She decided to bring buttons
> and thread to mend their clothes and touch their hearts. She
> convinced two of her friends to accompany her on the next
> trip: Kaye and Carole.
>
> For countless hours each day, Joan, Kaye, and Carole
> sat among the village children and sewed buttons onto their
> shirts, dresses, skirts, and pants. The women were barely visible
> in the middle of a sea of patient but expectant children who
> held out their ragged clothes asking, "May I have a button,
> please?" Carole's natural shyness provided the compassion
> required to coax some of the more reluctant children forward.
> Unfamiliar smells, dirt, coughs, and group pressure from hun-
> dreds of young bodies did not distract the three seamstresses
> from their task. Children walked miles from surrounding
> villages to seek not just new buttons but the kindness in each
> seamstress's voice, the softness of her touch. So prized was the

addition of one pretty button that a young girl tore a plain button off her dress and approached Joan to ask, "Button, please?" These three mothers traveled thousands of miles, not to conduct an evangelistic crusade, not even to teach a Vacation Bible School, but simply to sew buttons, compelled by the love of God.

The children of that Malawi village would have been robbed of these blessings if these women had not been willing to be themselves, to just be three moms who had sewn their share of buttons. For this assignment, all God needed was loving mothers.[2]

When I asked women what they would most want to hear in a book entitled *Let Your Life Count*, the number one answer was, "Tell me I can count right where I am, just as I am, that I don't have to be a missionary or world-changer, unless that's what God calls me to be. Tell me that living an ordinary life can count when I live it for an extraordinary God. Tell me that God is in the mundane just as powerfully as He is in the miraculous."

I'm writing to tell you just that.

Believe it or not, a pastor, evangelist, or Bible scholar is not always the right person for the job. Sometimes the right person is plain old ordinary you! (Not that I think you are ordinary, but you know what I mean! Too many of us underestimate our worth in God's kingdom.) God created you to be you and placed you on this earth with your skills, interests, and life experiences at this precise moment in time for a reason; don't thwart His plan. Be yourself.

What are some of your hobbies and skills? Not just your "super-spiritual" gifts, but your ordinary interests and experiences. What is your daily routine like? Turn everything over to God, and let Him show you how He wants to use *you*. If you want to let your life count, just be yourself. God created only one you, and only you can fulfill that role. Discover the freedom of yielding to God, and don't try to make your life count.

Remember

God created you to be you and placed you—with your skills, interests, and life experiences—at this precise moment in time for a reason; don't thwart His plan. Be yourself.

Reflect

What are some of your skills, interests, and life experiences that God might desire to work through? How have you seen God work through your life in the past?

Reach

Talk to some close friends and ask each of them to identify five unique things that make you "just you."

Compile a list and give special consideration to those
things that were mentioned by more than one person. Begin to pray, opening your heart to the ways
God might want to work through "just you."

---

*Dear heavenly Father, thank You for creating me exactly as I am and
placing me on this earth with my skills, interests, and life experiences at
this precise moment in time. I know I'm here for a reason. Lord, lead me
to people who can help me identify those characteristics that make me
truly unique. Sometimes it's so hard to see the good in me. Forgive me for
those times when I've tried to be someone I'm not, and empower me by
Your Holy Spirit to become all You've created me to be so that I can truly
let my life count. Amen.*

3

Don't Try to Make Your Life Count

Being confident of this, that he who began a good work
in you will carry it on to completion until the day of
Christ Jesus.

PHILIPPIANS 1:6

Okay, you are willing to just be yourself. You consider yourself
an ordinary person, but you still want your life to count. You
don't have a passport, so you know you won't be traipsing through
malaria-infested jungles anytime soon. But you picked up this book
because you want to make a difference in this world. Or maybe you're
thinking seriously about getting that passport and traipsing through
malaria-infested jungles. You're just not sure you have what it takes.
Either way, you're on the right track.

God created us with a desire to let our lives count, even as He created giraffes to eat the leaves off the tops of trees and the stars to twin-
kle at night. The desire to let our lives count is wired into every person;
it's what we were designed to do. It's what some psychologists have

called the search for significance—and it motivates much of what we do. We can respond in a variety of ways—some healthy, some unhealthy. The teenage girl walking around with 90 percent of her clothes missing is searching for significance. She thinks her life will count if she can get a guy to pay attention to her. The man trying to make lots of money, get that next promotion, or build his career or ministry is searching for significance. He thinks his life will count when he can dress well or get that pat on the back. The stay-at-home mom who screams at her kids when they don't behave perfectly is searching for significance. She thinks her life will count when she proves to the world that she's a great mother. Even the woman volunteering at her local church to run the biggest and best Vacation Bible School ever may well be yearning for significance. She thinks her life will count when the pastor mentions her from the pulpit.

The potential pitfall for those of us who want to count for God's kingdom comes when we shift gears from simply *letting* our lives count to frantically trying to *make* our lives count. Having made that very mistake—with painful and humiliating consequences—I felt it was important to warn you about it before we go any further on this journey together.

I realize that pondering word definitions is not the surefire way to launch a life-changing book. But I know that for me, understanding the difference between *letting* my life count and trying to *make* my life count has meant the difference between a nervous breakdown and finally figuring out just how simple God intended all of this to be. Few people have made more trips around the "God, let me show You what I can do" mountain than I have. So, alas, there's really no choice but to take a good, hard look at those two words, *letting* and *making,* but I pledge—on my honor as a recovering basket case—not to subject you to more visits to the dictionary than is absolutely necessary.

To let means "to allow, permit, agree to, or consent to." Essentially, it means "to yield, to give way."[1] To say, "Okay, have it Your way, God. I'm here and I'm open to whatever." *To make,* on the other hand, is all about driving ourselves and everyone around us bonkers, as in trying "to make things happen"—one of my personal specialties. It means "to create, build, craft, formulate, make up, knock together, manufacture, churn out, concoct, brew, earn, force to, compel to," and, my all-time favorite, "pressure somebody into."[2]

If you're anything like me, you have concocted numerous schemes to transform your household, compel your children to obey, earn brownie points with the boss, build a better church group, manufacture ministry opportunities, and brew up domestic accomplishments. Of course, such efforts exhaust me, so I then swing to other end of the spectrum. Perhaps this is where you live: curled up on the couch watching DVDs and eating Doritos, refusing to get in on the game of life because you're convinced you will never amount to anything anyway.

It's also important to clarify what the distinction between *letting your life count* and *trying to make your life count* doesn't mean. It doesn't mean that anyone who is active in ministry must be on the wrong track or is trying to make something happen. Nor does it mean that the truly spiritual people are sitting around doing nothing, thereby enabling God to do everything for them.

You've probably seen the classic movie *Chariots of Fire.* If not, I encourage you to do so because it paints a powerful portrait of two Olympic runners: Harold Abrahams, who tried desperately to *make* his life count by winning a gold medal, and Eric Liddell, who in humble obedience to God simply *let* his life count by winning a race he wasn't even qualified to run. Both men achieved the same outcome (that is, they each went home with a gold medal, though in separate races), but their experiences of the process were completely different. One made himself and everyone around him miserable; the other was a blessing to every life he touched. That's because Harold Abrahams was running in search of significance, while Eric Liddell was running because he believed God wanted to do something significant through his life.

Cec Murphey, writer of numerous award-winning books, lives by this motto: "I am passionately involved in the process and emotionally detached from the results."[3] These words clarify how we can discover whether we are looking to ourselves or looking to God in our desire for significance. Are we trying to make our lives count, or are we letting our lives count? How do we respond when we take a step of faith and everything doesn't turn out the way we had hoped? How attached are we to a specific outcome? Are we just happy to be of serv-

If you struggle with finding balance between *letting* and *making* your life count, you can listen to an encouraging online message, "Accepting Yourself Without Excusing Yourself," by visiting www.donnapartow.com and clicking the link for free Audios.

ice, or are we determined that our service yield the results we envision, especially if those results are "successful" events—a higher position in the church, admiration, a new best friend, or well-mannered children? If we are frustrated, angry, depressed, or otherwise upset, it's probably because we were overly attached to the outcome.

Jane had done everything that could be done to serve at her local church. "I've taught Sunday school, organized Vacation Bible School, decorated the church with poinsettias for Christmas, planned the annual mother-daughter tea party. You name it, I've run it." But despite the whirlwind of church activity, Jane felt empty inside. Perpetually exhausted, she felt overworked and underappreciated. She knew something was wrong.

Then one Sunday her pastor preached on "getting in the flow of God." He explained that ministry might be physically draining, but when you are doing what God created you to do, it should be energizing, as well. He suggested that if your service to God left you routinely exhausted, you probably weren't in the flow of what God created you to do.

Jane said, "I was trying *too hard* to make my life count. I was sitting around thinking up stuff I could do for God, when all I really needed to do was get in the flow of what God wanted to do through me. It sounds so obvious now, but I had spent thirty years getting it backwards."

Jane met with her pastor, and they agreed she should relinquish all her responsibilities for a while. He proposed that she consider a time when her service left her more energized than exhausted. "He asked me what I could do, and do joyfully, even if no one ever noticed or acknowledged my effort. What activity brought me satisfaction, in and of itself, in the midst of the journey, not just when all was said and done and everyone applauded my efforts?"

Jane took what she called a radical sabbatical from volunteering and spent extended time praying, journaling about her dreams, and reflecting on past ministry involvement. In the end, she decided to volunteer as a math tutor at an outreach center targeting underprivileged kids. "As crazy as this sounds, I *love* teaching kids math. I *love* watching them work through problems and seeing those moments when a giant light bulb goes on over a kid's head and I know he finally gets it." She says tutoring does indeed bring joy rather exhaustion. "I don't have to work at this; it's fun, it fits!"

When Jane stopped doing things she thought would count and started doing the thing that brought her joy, she discovered she could do what she loved for the glory of God. Notice, however, that her journey to her God-ordained place of significance began on her knees. If we desire to let our lives count, we'll begin in the same way as we discover God-directed prayer.

The potential pitfall for those of us who want to let our lives count comes when we shift gears from simply *letting* to frantically trying to *make* our lives count. Your life can count when you forget trying to make something happen and simply let your life be available to God.

Reflect

Which side of the pendulum do you tend to swing toward: trying too hard to make something happen or refusing to get in on the game of life? Why do you think that is?

Reach

If you're on the frantic side, list one activity you need to cease (because you now realize it's something you're concocting, brewing, or manufacturing). Now take a specific step to bring it to an end. If you're on the passive side, ask God to show you one small way you can become more available for Him.

Dear heavenly Father, I sincerely want to let my life count. I recognize the potential pitfall of shifting gears from simply letting my life count to frantically trying to make it count. We both know I've made that mistake before with unfortunate results! Holy Spirit, please help me not feel condemned because of foolish things I've done in a headlong rush to make something happen. Forgive me, too, for those opportunities I've missed because I was unwilling to get in on the game of life. I just want to be available to You. I invite You to show me if there is anything I need to stop or start doing so I can be more available to You. Amen.

4

Discover God-Directed Prayer

This is the confidence we have in approaching God: that if we ask anything according to his will, he hears us. And if we know that he hears us—whatever we ask—we know that we have what we asked of him.

1 JOHN 5:14–15

When I'm speaking at a conference, I often begin my session on prayer with a game I've dubbed Guess the Gift. Here's how it works. I randomly select a woman from the audience and inform her that I have a gift for someone else in the room. Her challenge is to guess two things: whom the gift is for, and what it is. After a few tries, the woman *and the audience* usually become frustrated as they realize the absurdity of the game. Then I suggest we change the rules a bit. "How about if you just *ask me* whom the gift is for and what the gift is? Would that be a little easier?" Relieved, the woman says yes and then asks me whom the gift is for and what it is.

I tell her. She gives the gift to the happy recipient, and peace is restored to all concerned.

I play this game to illustrate how many of us approach prayer. The Bible says, "Your Father knows what you need before you ask him" (Matthew 6:8). God knows what people truly need, *and* He has the resources to meet those needs. Not only that, He also knows what's on their gift lists, their wish lists, and even their wildest-dreams lists. God is a gift giver who gives much better gifts than we possibly could. In fact, "Every good and perfect gift is from above" (James 1:17).

God doesn't need us to play Guess the Gift. When we come to Him in prayer, we can just ask Him, *Lord, what gifts do You have today? And whom are they for? Whom do You want to bless today? How can I be part of someone's answer to prayer?* In other words, God is simply looking for delivery people!

Too often, we spend our prayer times trying to tell God what gifts He should give or what He should do in people's lives. *Okay, God, Bob needs a new job, Judy needs You to heal her foot, Susan needs a new car, Karl needs his daughter to move back home, Kristi needs money for her short-term missions trip, the church needs money for the building fund, and I need my husband to be nicer to me.* On and on we go, babbling like pagans—the very thing Jesus told us *not* to do (Matthew 6:7).

Meanwhile, God is saying, *Yes, child, you've guessed one right today. Susan needs a car—that's on My list, and I wanted to talk about how you can cooperate with Me to help deliver that car to her.* Of course, we won't be able to hear God if we're too busy babbling. In prayer, as in life, it's hard to listen when we are talking. Many times we don't even try to listen; we're quickly moving on to the next item on our lists because, frankly, we never expected to get answers, and we certainly didn't expect to *be* part of the answers. (And we wonder why we don't sense that our lives count!)

Effective prayer consists not in telling God what to do but in listening as He tells us what He wants to do. One of the reasons so many prayers seem to go unanswered is because our prayer lists are too much like shopping lists. We fail to realize that *God has the real prayer list.*

That's right: *God has the real prayer list.*

Your life can count, and your life will count, when you put away *your* prayer list so you can discover what's on *God's* prayer list. The prayers that begin with God's heart—the prayers we feel *prompted* or *burdened* to pray—aren't those prayers always answered, often in truly miraculous ways that count for eternity? Of course they are!

I had just finished speaking on the subject of God-directed prayer when a small, gray-haired woman walked up to me with tears streaming down her face and asked if she could tell me her story. She said that she and her husband were serving as missionaries in Africa when he contracted severe malaria. One night he called her into the bedroom, informing her that he didn't expect to survive until morning. He explained what she needed to know about the work and about the children's futures. Then the couple said their farewells to each other through tears.

Meanwhile in California, a friend of theirs was awakened in the middle of the night, burdened to pray for these missionaries. Fortunately this woman had learned to recognize and respond to God's prayer promptings. That night the prompting was so strong that she noted the date and the hour when she was awakened and felt led to pray. She remained on her knees until the burden lifted the next morning, and she wrote down the time when she finished praying. The experience was so powerful that she wrote to the missionaries, inquiring what had been happening during that time frame. When the couple received the letter several weeks later, they saw that God had awakened their friend at the very hour the missionary had called his wife to his bedside. They also realized that their friend had remained on her knees until the missionary's fever had broken the next morning. By noon, he had been out of danger.

I believe God healed the missionary because this woman prayed. Jesus wasn't joking when He said *pray* that God's kingdom will come and that His will be done here on earth (Matthew 6:10). He told us to pray *because our prayers are essential.* God's acting is contingent upon our asking! God actively seeks prayer partners. When He wants to *intervene* in human affairs, His eyes range throughout all the earth, searching for someone who will *intercede,* thereby inviting Him to act.

John Wesley said, "God does nothing but in answer to believing prayer."[1] Did you catch that? Nothing! Yet less than one in ten thousand American Christians pray an hour a day.[2] Church leaders think it's difficult to get people to tithe their *money;* have you ever stopped to consider how much a tithe of your *time* would be? Quick, do the math! That's right: two and a half hours per day. How many people do you know who offer God a tithe in prayer of their daily twenty-four hours? Now, before you panic because this sounds impossible, hang in there with me. The next chapter offers a reasonable and practical answer to this challenge.

I've been privileged to know a few mighty prayer warriors, but they *are* few. Perhaps that's because many of us think John Wesley got it wrong. We don't believe that "God does *nothing* but in answer to *believing* prayer" (emphasis added). In fact, many Western Christians are convinced that God's kingdom operates entirely apart from our involvement—apparently all we're doing is marking time until Jesus comes back. We're unwilling to give God two and a half hours of our days in prayer because we don't think our prayers are necessary to God's work in the world. Many Christians believe we should pray just because Christ commanded it or because we want to cultivate our relationship with God. In the movie *Shadowlands,* C. S. Lewis declared, "Prayer does not change God, prayer changes me." Corrie ten Boom wrote an entire book around her conviction that in prayer we obtain our marching orders from God.[3]

I would like to take these truths a step further. Prayer does more than change us; it does more than inform us; prayer *changes the world.* My favorite author on the subject of prayer is E. M. Bounds. He was a pastor during the American Civil War and is widely considered the greatest authority on prayer in the two-thousand-year history of the church. He claimed that:

The prayers of God's saints are the capital stock in heaven
by which Christ carries on His great work upon earth....
The very life and prosperity of God's cause—even its very

existence—depend on prayer.... Our Lord's kingdom is *dependent upon prayer....* We neglect it—not only to our own spiritual hurt, but also to the delay and injury of our Lord's cause upon earth.[4] (emphasis added)

E. M. Bounds was convinced that if the church won't pray, God won't act, that God has literally chosen to limit His actions on this earth to those things He accomplishes through the prayers of His people. Do you believe that? You may say you do, but what does your prayer life say about your beliefs?

I wonder what our private lives and public church services would look like if we were convinced that God actually directs the affairs of the world through the prayers of His people. Jesus said *to the church,* "I'm standing at the door knocking. Would someone *please* open the door and invite me in?" (Revelation 3:20, paraphrased). What if we were convinced that God's *acting* is contingent upon our *asking*?

I realize this perspective on prayer differs from the common conviction that while prayer is a wonderful religious exercise, our prayerlessness certainly cannot inhibit God. He's going to do whatever He wants to do, whether or not we pray. However, I would encourage you to study Scripture on the matter and consider whether or not this is so. Charles Spurgeon, the prince of preachers, concluded that Scripture does indeed tie God's intervention with our requests:

Whether we like it or not, asking is the rule of the kingdom. "Ask and ye shall receive" (John 16:24). It is a rule that never will be altered in anybody's case.... God [the Father] has not relaxed the rule even for…His own Son, "Ask of me, and I shall give thee the heathen for thine inheritance" (Psalm 2:8).… If the royal and divine Son of God cannot be exempted from the rule of asking…you and I cannot expect the rule to be relaxed in our favor. Why should it be?…

God will bless Elijah and send rain on Israel, but Elijah must pray for it. If the chosen nation is to prosper, Samuel must plead for it. If the Jews are to be delivered, Daniel must intercede. God will bless Paul, and the nations will be converted through him, but Paul must pray…without ceasing.[5]

Most church members can be divided into two distinct groups: those who pray for an hour or more a day and those who rarely pray. People who pray for extended lengths of time do so not because of age, race, gender, denomination, or even years of church attendance but because they've seen answers to prayer and they know their prayers count. People who have *not seen* answers to prayer and who *do not believe* their prayers count rarely pray with such fervency. In fact, I'm convinced the number one hindrance to prayer is unanswered prayer. It's a vicious cycle: we don't pray because we've prayed before but nothing happened, so we don't pray, so nothing happens—so we don't pray!

Of course, some of us take the middle road of routine, perfunctory prayer. We don't really believe prayer counts for much of anything, but, hey, what have we got to lose? Just like the gambler who keeps throwing the dice, we keep throwing prayers into the air. We reason that someone's got to win and someone's got to get the occasional answer to prayer. Maybe we'll be the lucky ones! Besides, we can experience the temporary elation of checking *Pray* off our daily to-do lists.

E. M. Bounds calls this "prayerless praying," and he went so far as to say, "Better not to pray at all than to go through a dead form that secures no answer, brings no glory to God and supplies no good to man. Nothing so hardens the heart and nothing so blinds us to the unseen and the eternal, as this kind of prayerless praying."[6]

Scripture clearly teaches that prayers are meant to be answered; they are not simply meant to keep us occupied (see Jeremiah 33:3, Psalm 91:15, and Matthew 7:7–8). The key is: where do our prayers originate? "This is the confidence we have in approaching God: that if we ask anything according to his will, he hears us" (1 John 5:14). His will. His heart. His agenda. His prayer list. That's where it all begins.

Does that mean we can never ask for things we want? Certainly not. As God's beloved children, we're invited to walk boldly into His throne room anytime, day or night, and make our requests known. However, if we want our prayer times—and our lifetimes—to count,

For more on God-directed prayer, listen online to "Prayer: The Gathering of Gifts" at no charge. Visiting www.donna partow.com and click the link for Audios. You can also join Prayer Force, which features weekly teachings on prayer, resources to enhance your prayer life, and suggestions for further study. Visit www.donnapartow.com/prayer_force.

it just makes sense to become God's prayer partner rather than to ask Him to become ours. It just makes sense to get in alignment with His will rather than to beg Him to get on board with our plans.

When we pray according to God's heart, our prayers truly make a difference; they count in God's spiritual economy. Prayer is the only established means by which we invite the presence of God into the world—and God does *not* show up uninvited. He does nothing apart from our asking—or someone's asking on our behalf. Our prayers then, in a very real sense, form a bridge that links heaven and earth. When it comes to answered prayer, God is counting on *you*!

Am I saying we should never pray unless God wakes us up in the middle of the night? that we should never write down our prayer requests? Absolutely not. However, *God should lead* our prayer times. Far better to pray with a blank notebook asking God, *What's on Your heart, heavenly Father? What's on Your prayer list?* Then as He brings areas of concern to mind, we can sit silently and begin filling our notebooks with prayer concerns.

I've found this approach to prayer to be extremely meaningful, powerful, and effective, even in a group setting. One Tuesday night, for example, my prayer team and I asked God to direct our prayers, and He led us to pray for many nations of the world rather than to pray for any personal concerns. On other occasions, He has prompted us to pray almost exclusively for one individual. Incidentally, we pray with our Bibles on our laps because we find that God often leads us to specific passages of Scripture through which He desires to speak.

One prerequisite for effective, God-directed prayers is to broaden our circles of concern and make it a priority to stay well-informed about the work of God's kingdom around the world. It would have been hard (though certainly not impossible) for God to lead that California woman to pray for the missionary couple if she didn't know and care about them. Of course, the more actively we engage ourselves in the world around us, the more people and situations we will know, and the more likely God is to call upon us as *His* prayer partners. The more time we spend sitting in silence before Him, with the Word of God opened, the more clearly we will hear His heart through God-directed prayers.

Marisol literally became one of God's delivery people in response to His prompting. A brand-new mother with a wide circle of friends, she had received far more baby gifts than she needed. "I was going to return some stuff to the store and get a store credit to purchase things at another time," she said. But then she remembered her promise to God not to make any decision, small or large, without consulting Him first. As she prayed, God led her in a completely different direction: *Why not give these new things away to some young mother who would normally get used items?* The next Sunday there was a notice in the bulletin about a local crisis pregnancy center.

Marisol made an appointment to drop off the items. Unknown to her, the center had been fasting and praying specifically for a volunteer who was fluent in Spanish. When the director mentioned the need to Marisol (who was born in Puerto Rico), she had no interest whatsoever. "I politely took the brochure and left. As I was walking away from the center, I stuck the brochure in my pocket and said to myself, 'Yeah, right.' I didn't want anything to do with such a controversial issue." This time, it was God who gently reminded her of the promise she had made. So she went home and prayed for direction: *Lord, is this something You want me to do? I don't want to do it. I don't know anything about it. I don't have any skills for it, and frankly, I'd rather not. But I will if You want me to. Just let me know, and please don't be subtle because I might miss it! Make sure You're loud and clear.*

A couple weeks later, Marisol hopped in the car, turned on the ignition, and the radio came *blasting* over the airwaves. It was Dr. James Dobson making an impassioned plea for Christians to get involved in crisis pregnancy ministries. Marisol had to laugh. When she asked God to make it *loud* and clear, He had taken her literally! Trembling, she reached in her coat pocket and pulled out the brochure. She called, and a prayer was answered. She says, "I shudder when I think of the blessings I would've missed if I hadn't stopped to consult Him first."

As an orphanage director once said to a group of volunteers, "You are here because one of the little children prayed, *Daddy, help me!* and God reached across the world to find the right hearts and the right people. In most cases, they are people who had already been praying, *Daddy, help the children.* He heard both prayers and built a bridge."

We miss out on so much joy in this world because we're so focused on ourselves and our agendas, even when we pray. Instead, simply *listen* as God directs you, not only to pray, but perhaps to be part of the answer. If you want to let your life count, discover the joy of God-directed prayer and begin to live daily in God's presence.

Remember

Effective prayer consists not in telling God what to do but in listening as He tells us what He wants to do. One of the reasons many prayers go unanswered is because our prayer lists are too much like shopping lists. We fail to realize that *God has the real prayer list.* Let God direct your prayer time!

Reflect

Think of a time when you felt prompted, or even burdened, to pray. Did you see that prayer answered in a dramatic way? What difference have you noticed between prayer-list-driven prayer and God-directed prayer?

Reach

Obtain a blank notebook and gather up your Bible. Set aside some time to sit quietly with God's Word open upon your lap, and ask Him to lead your prayer time. After you have done this several times and are comfortable doing so, introduce God-directed praying to a group of fellow believers (whether a Sunday-school class, small group, or informal group of friends).

Dear heavenly Father, I'm so thankful that I don't need to compile prayer lists to keep You informed about what's going on in the world! You already know, and You have the real prayer list. Lord, I want to be Your prayer partner and to pray for the gifts and gift recipients that You want me to pray for today. I want to be the one who delivers hope to the hopeless, healing to the hurting, encouragement to the discouraged, compassion to the one who has stumbled. Holy Spirit, I open my spirit ears to You now. Speak to me, Lord, for Your child is here and ready to hear. Amen.

5

Live Daily in God's Presence

Then Moses said to him, "If your Presence does not go
with us, do not send us up from here."

Exodus 33:15

I know what some of you are thinking after reading the last
chapter. *Pray two and a half hours a day? Is this woman crazy?
Who on earth has time to sit and pray for that long?* But let me ask you
this: how many hours a day are you awake? When praying becomes
like breathing, you can pray during every waking hour.

Many Christians believe in a false dichotomy: *either* we sit and
pray *or* we go out into the world, helping people and taking care of
our daily routines. But prayer is not an either/or proposition. As my
mother-in-law always says, "We pray as we go." It's called practicing
the presence of God.

Brother Lawrence, the seventeenth-century monk whose collected
letters and essays comprise the enduring book *The Practice of the Presence of God,* claimed, "To think that you must abandon communion

with Him in order to deal with the world is erroneous."[1] In fact, quite the opposite is true. To deal with the world and all its demands effectively, we must *maintain* communion with God as we go about our routine tasks. It's a simple matter of living with a conscious awareness of God, silently communicating with Him as we would with an everpresent friend. As we live our days in God's presence, we'll discover that in His presence is fullness of joy; in fact, there is joy unspeakable (see Psalm 16:11).

But that's not all. Our lives will also become infused with new power and purpose. The power in the Christian life does not come from knowing about God. It doesn't come from having a lot of Bible knowledge or from memorizing Scripture. Those things are important, but it's God's presence that brings God's power into our lives, including the power for us to live holy lives and the power to inspire change in the life of every person we encounter.[2]

Jackson Senyonga, pastor of the largest church in Uganda (which is currently experiencing a powerful spiritual revival) has observed that, "In the presence of God, the possibility for miracles always exists."[3] Senyonga urges American Christians who want to make a difference in this country to "cultivate the presence of God" and to "create an atmosphere in our hearts and homes where the spirit of God feels welcome."[4]

Let me tell you a story that illustrates the impact of atmosphere. In the late 1990s I moved into a cedar-sided cabin on the side of a little mountain and owned two goats named Mark and Luke. They ate everything in sight, especially the stuff they weren't supposed to eat, like my roses. My goats weren't particularly useful; I couldn't milk them, as you probably guessed by their names! I loved them anyway.

My favorite time of day was our morning climb. I would wake up, usually to the sound of our roosters crowing. I'd feed the chickens and ducks, water my garden, and then I would let the goats out of their pen and start leading the way to the mountaintop. Each day I hoped against hope that *this* was the day we would climb without resistance, without delays or detours.

Those days were rare indeed, because the house next door was perpetually under construction. Like most construction sites, it was an eternal trash heap: foam coffee cups, fast-food restaurant wrappings, wood scraps, nails. My goats found that trash heap simply irresistible. Sometimes all I had to do was coax them back onto the path. Sometimes I would bribe them with their favorite honey-and-grain mix. Some days I actually picked up Mark, the lead goat, because I knew Luke would follow. Then there were days when I took a tree limb and did some serious persuasion.

Why didn't I just leave those goats alone to enjoy their trash heap? Because I happened to know that they were *not* trash heap goats; they were *mountain goats*. I knew that despite all their protests, once we got to the top of that mountain, those goats would be filled with joy. They would leap from rock to rock, butting their little heads together. Then they would do something that they would not do at any other place or any other time. They would come and lay their heads down on my lap, and we would experience a special closeness that otherwise eluded us. They would snuggle up to me as if to say, *How can we thank you enough for reminding us of who we really are?* Somehow they had been temporarily deceived into believing they were merely trash heap goats; now they remembered that God created them to be mountain goats.

One day as we sat together on the top of that mountain, I realized, *I'm just like these goats!* So often I choose to live in the trash heap of life, rather than drawing close to God. He wants to remind me who I really am. I wasn't created to live in the trash heap of life; I was created to enjoy living in His presence. But I fight Him tooth and nail. Even though I know the tranquillity I experience when I climb higher to fellowship with God, I still ignore His call.

The trash heap my goats liked to pillage through was mostly fast-food restaurant wrappings and other junk the workers had thrown away. Just stuff. My goats weren't distracted by anything "bad" or "evil." The same is true for most of us. We're rummaging around in trash heaps, whether it's the garbage in our minds (bitterness, anger, escapism) or meddling in other people's business. We fail to realize how the garbage of gossip, envy, a critical spirit, or a judgmental attitude pollutes the atmosphere of our lives. God cannot work in an atmosphere where His Spirit is grieved. That's why we're told to put away all "bitterness, rage and anger, brawling and slander, along with every form of malice" (Ephesians 4:31).

Granted, we can live in the trash heap and still keep ourselves occupied doing things that are supposedly *for God,* but that's exactly what we need to *stop doing!* Because so often when we're busy doing things for God, we're unavailable to let God do His work through us.

We were meant to be mountaintop people—to live where the atmosphere of our spirits is pure and refreshing to our souls and to all we encounter. We were meant to walk with God. When we journey with Him daily to higher ground, we discover the presence-driven life. We begin to pray, to read God's Word, to obey His commands, simply because we long to be in His presence. We learn that we can be in God's presence, not just on the mountaintops of life, but moment by moment. We take the mountaintop atmosphere with us wherever we go.

One of the simplest and most practical ways to practice the presence of God throughout the day is to let your daily life become a series of opportunities for drawing your mind back to a conscious awareness of God. As you let your daily life remind you to turn to Him in prayer, however briefly, you will be reminded of His presence and His active involvement in the world.

One important proviso: the following starting-points-for-prayer are suggestions, exactly that and nothing more. I will have defeated the entire purpose of this chapter if these become set prayer lists or if we deteriorate into praying *our agendas.* Instead, these are examples of how God has led me to pray in the past. As you remain open to God-directed prayers, He will lead you well beyond these brief ideas.

Food and drink. If you were to pray a quick prayer every time you opened your mouth to put something in it, you would dramatically increase the amount of time you devote to prayer each day. Every morsel of food and every sip of water can serve as reminders of God's loving care for you. If you drink eight glasses of water a day (and I hope you do) and thank God for every sip, you'll become a powerful prayer warrior overnight!

Begin with simple, childlike faith: *Thank You, Father, for this food. Thank You for clean water. You are so good to me. Help me to cultivate a more thankful heart.* You can ask God for wisdom concerning your eating habits: *Help me to make wise food choices and to care for my body, which is the temple of the Holy Spirit.* You might even pray, *Lord, help me understand why I'm craving this doughnut right now!*

As you become comfortable with simple prayers of gratitude, move to interceding for others: *Lord, as I drink this water, I can't help thinking about the billions of people on this planet who don't have access to safe drinking water. Bless them today. Lay it on the hearts of Your people to assist them. I thank You for World Vision. Bless their staff today as they install wells around the world. Show me and show my church how we can make a difference.*

If you are in a restaurant, ask your waitperson how you can pray for him or her today. I have always had people respond favorably to this offer. One young man even knelt down by the table and allowed us to pray for him on the spot. He got up with tears in his eyes. (However, before taking this step, you must promise me you will leave an excellent tip of 20 percent or more! I do not think it's possible for us, as Christians, to be too generous with those who wait upon us.)

Possessions. God is our provider, and He deserves our thanks. When you get dressed in the morning, thank God for each article of clothing as you put it on. You might also use each item as a reminder of the "full armor of God" (Ephesians 6:11–17). As you put on your hat to go out the door, thank God for the helmet of salvation; as you put on your shoes, ask God to empower you to walk in the gospel of peace, and so on. If you want, you can declare your purse the sword of the Spirit—then make that a reality by arming yourself with a travel Bible, scripture-verse cards, and tracts such as the "Four Spiritual

Laws." As you sit down at your kitchen table for breakfast, thank God for your home, your furniture, the safety of your environment, and so on. As you enter your car, thank God for it and ask Him to keep you safe and to grant you divine appointments throughout the day.

Phone calls. Before dialing or answering the phone, ask God to bless your conversation. Pray that He will give you the right words so that whatever you say will benefit those who listen. "Do not let any unwholesome talk come out of your mouths, but only what is helpful for building others up according to their needs, that it may *benefit those* who listen" (Ephesians 4:29, emphasis added). Pray verse 3 of Psalm 141: "Set a guard over my mouth, O LORD; keep watch over the door of my lips."

Once the habit of praying before phone conversations is firmly established, you might develop the practice of asking the other party if and how you might pray for her before you hang up the phone. If you want to write down the prayer request, you may do so. But what's more important is to pray right then. This is an excellent way to end conversations. It is an especially gracious way to signal to a distressed

You can learn more on this topic by listening online to "In His Presence." Visit www.donnapartow.com and click the link for free Audios. If you haven't done so already, visit our Let Your Life Count Community at www.donnapartow .com/lylc_community to share your adventures as you implement the suggestions in this chapter.

person that you *do care* even though you need to hang up so you can proceed with other obligations.

When you hang up the phone, ask God to erase the memory of any words you may have spoken that might be misinterpreted or harmful and to seal those words you spoke that were ordained by Him.

Personal encounters. Whether you have a planned meeting with a friend at the park so your children can play together or you notice an acquaintance across a parking lot, when you first set eyes on someone you know, *pray* God's blessing upon her life. Ask God to bless your time together and to make you sensitive to her needs. Next, develop the habit of asking everyone you spend time with how you can pray for her. As you become more comfortable with a lifestyle of prayer, offer to pray aloud before departing from one another's presence. Eventually, you may develop the practice of opening and ending every encounter with a brief prayer.

One of the easiest ways to forget about your own problems is to stay alert to people around you who are clearly having either a tough day or a tough life. Many people wear their heartaches openly. Pray for them as you pass by. I was once trying on some clothing and noticed that the young woman helping me seemed upset. I inquired, and it turned out she was scheduled for surgery later that week. When I offered to keep her in my prayers, she was visibly moved. I have never, ever had a stranger respond negatively to my offer to simply pray for her (as opposed to trying to evangelize her—which many people are offended by!).

Silent prayers can be just as effective. Two particular silent prayers stand out in my mind. In the first instance, a man was ranting and raving at the gate agent in an airport. I walked over, laid my hands on him, and gently stroked his back while praying silently. He immediately calmed down. I then offered to give him my seat on the plane. Another time, I had a layover at the Las Vegas airport on a return trip from Canada. It was late Sunday night, and many people were clearly wired from a weekend of gambling and partying. I noticed one particularly boisterous young man covered in pentagram tattoos (the symbol of Satanism). His T-shirt read, "Satan is my ^@(&@* co-pilot." So I sat down beside him and struck up a conversation. Much to my amazement, he didn't resist at all when I laid my hand on his and began silently praying as I simply smiled at him. He immediately calmed down, as had the other man, and we talked for over an hour. It turned out I was waiting at the wrong gate and missed my flight home. But was it really the wrong gate?

Not long ago, my husband, Jeff, saw a man who had parked his motorcycle by the side of the road and displayed a sign reading Free Prayer. Jeff passed him twice, and the motorcycle man had a line of customers both times. No kidding! If that doesn't tell you something about how open people are to prayer, I'm out of inspirational stories!

Churches. We'd like to believe that churches are nice, safe places where everyone sings campfire songs all day long. The reality is that they are spiritual war zones and that the pastoral staff must face many battles each day. Pray for every church as you pass. Bless the pastor and his family—for strength, unity, safety, and peace. Pray for wisdom for those in leadership, for the fire of God to fall upon the congregation, and for peace among those who may be quarrelling. If the churches have outdoor message boards promoting upcoming events, pray specifically for

God's blessings upon them. Pray that the churches make an impact on the community. It's sad to think how many churches could close their doors tomorrow and no one in the surrounding neighborhood (other than the members) would even notice. Pray for a spirit of outreach.

Schools. As you drop your children off at school, pray for and with them. Pray for their classmates, that each child would grow "in wisdom and stature, and in favor with God and men" (Luke 2:52). Pray that God would lead and guide the teachers as they teach and the staff as they run the affairs of the school. Pray that the fire of revival would fall upon the students and that God would do mighty things in their generation. Eventually, you might want to go beyond these brief prayers and make it a point to spend extra time each day (or one day a week) praying as you walk around the campus or sit in your car in the parking lot.

Even if you homeschool your children or if you don't have school-aged children, you can still pray every time you drive past a school or school bus. Pray God's blessings upon the education system and upon the students and teachers. Pray for the countless millions of children around the world who do not have educational opportunities. Ask God to open doors for Christians to operate schools and orphanages around the world, and ask God to open the hearts of Christians to be willing to use their teaching gifts in nations where the needs are greatest. Having worked with many missionaries, I would add that we should *all pray daily* for the educational needs of missionary kids (MKs, as they are commonly called), as this is a constant source of concern for missionary families.

Community. Each time you drive past a government building, police station, fire department, library, and so on, pray for our nation and for the men and women who serve in our communities. Pray for their safety and prosperity. Whenever you see a police car, pray for the officer behind the wheel and for policemen everywhere. When an ambulance or fire engine goes flying past you, take time to pray for those who are in harm's way and for those who have devoted their lives to the safety of our communities.

You might take this a step further and bake cookies for the local police and fire departments. Include a note that lets them know you are praying for them.

Offensive images. If Christians prayed for God's divine intervention in the media every time they saw something offensive—either on a magazine rack, on television, or on the Internet—we would soon see dramatic changes in the cultural atmosphere. Pray for God to touch the hearts of key media decision makers and for Him to open doors for Christians to create more positive images and messages. Pray against evil influences and ask God to protect the innocence of our children, keeping them safe from the damaging effects of violent and pornographic images. Pray for the safety and effectiveness of Christians who are fighting against these destructive forces.

Anxious thoughts. Even though this and the following items are actually *the most important* and *powerful* ways to practice the presence of God, I've saved them for last because they are perhaps the most difficult for the average person to incorporate into daily life. However, if you first practice the simple items just described, your approach to life will have changed so dramatically that you will find developing these challenging spiritual disciplines much easier.

Among the most powerful ways to practice the presence of God is taking "captive every thought" (2 Corinthians 10:5)—especially every anxious, angry, bitter, worrisome, or negative thought. As soon as you realize that your mind is occupied with negative thoughts, immediately turn those thoughts into a prayer. Very often, Christians will either entertain those thoughts or push them away. A third alternative is best: capture the thoughts and then turn them into a prayer. For example, if you catch yourself worrying about your teenager, turn that into a prayer: *Heavenly Father, I thank You that my children are not my own; they are Yours. I pray, right now, that You will guard my child, surrounding her with favor as with a shield, causing her to discern good from evil. I thank You for Your promise that the children of the upright will be blessed.* Pray for your child's activities, friends, attitudes, and opportunities. Pray healing over her past and hope for her future. Practicing the presence of God means living in the moment. Rather than dwelling on the past or worrying about the future, turning anxious thoughts into prayers brings you into the present where God can transform you.

As you begin to acknowledge what you're thinking about, you'll be able to "take captive every thought to make it obedient to Christ" (2 Corinthians 10:5). Specifically, you'll become obedient to the command: "Finally, brothers, whatever is true, whatever is noble, whatever is right, whatever is pure, whatever is lovely, whatever is admirable— if anything is excellent or praiseworthy—think about such things" (Philippians 4:8). If you are anything like me, turning negative thoughts into prayers will result in far more than two and a half hours of prayer a day. (For more assistance with this area, I suggest my previous books, *Soon to Be a Major Motion Picture: New Direction for Life's Dramas* and *Becoming the Woman I Want to Be: A 90-Day Journey to Renewing Spirit, Soul, and Body*.)

Morning and evening devotions. Many of you already have incorporated a morning or evening devotional time into your daily routine. Even if you haven't established the habit, you have surely heard more than enough sermons on the topic. I won't belabor the obvious here. However, I do want to emphasize that this spiritual discipline has absolutely nothing to do with crossing a task off your to-do list or earning brownie points with God. It is vital to your *own spiritual well-being* to establish the right atmosphere around you when you first awake and before retiring for the evening. There's something both joyous and liberating about deliberately giving God your day—both before it begins and as it comes to an end. When you awake, ask Him to walk with you and show you how He wants to work through you. Surrender your agenda. Then, the last thing you should do before your head hits the pillow is surrender the day to Him—the good, the bad, and the ugly—so you can sleep well and wake refreshed.

Truly, we need time with God both in the morning and in the evening—not for God's sake, but again, for our souls' well-being. In my view, fifteen minutes morning *and* evening is better than thirty minutes in the morning without giving thought to how you lived your life or casting your cares upon your heavenly Father before going to sleep at night.

To that end, it's helpful to have a specific devotional book you are reading through in addition to God's Word. Some of my favorites are

- *Come Away My Beloved* by Frances J. Roberts
- *Daily in Your Presence* by Rebecca Barlow Jordan
- *Face to Face* by Kenneth Boa
- *Morning and Evening* by Charles Spurgeon
- *My Utmost for His Highest* by Oswald Chambers (updated edition by James Reimann)
- *Streams in the Desert* by L. B. Cowman (updated edition by James Reimann)

You might begin to incorporate the preceding ideas one at a time. For example, once thanking God for everything that goes into your mouth becomes second nature, begin thanking Him as you make use of the possessions He has graciously provided. Then develop the habit of praying before, during, and after phone calls, and so on. Eventually, you will discover that you are mindful of God all day long and that practicing His presence has become like breathing; prayer becomes your atmosphere!

As you practice the presence of God, praying as you go throughout your day, you not only take God with you everywhere you go, you'll discover He is already there ahead of you, as we will see in the next chapter.

Remember

In the presence of God, the possibility for miracles always exists. We can walk in the presence and power of God even as we go about our daily routines.

Reflect

Do you take time in the morning to "climb the mountain"—that is, to spend time in God's presence? Which of the suggested prayer cues might work most effectively for you?

Reach

Prayerfully consider some practical ways you can increase your awareness of God's presence throughout the day. The most powerful steps you can take are beginning your day on the mountaintop with God and cultivating there an awareness of God that you can then carry with you as you go.

Dear heavenly Father, I thank You that in Your presence the possibility for miracles always exists. Help me to walk, moment by moment, with a conscious awareness of Your presence and an active involvement in the world around me. Holy Spirit, draw me to the mountaintop with You. And help me to carry the atmosphere of the mountaintop with me throughout the day. Amen.

6

You Were Created to Be a Sign That God Cares

He comes alongside us when we go through hard times,
and before you know it, he brings us alongside someone
else who is going through hard times so that we can be
there for that person just as God was there for us.

2 CORINTHIANS 1:4 (MSG)

The first four letters in the word *significance* provide a powerful clue to our purpose as children of God: *s-i-g-n*. We were created to be a sign, to signify God to the world. A sign can simply indicate the existence of something. For example, scientists search for signs of life on Mars, and doctors look for signs or symptoms of various illnesses. When hunters find fresh deer tracks in the forest, the tracks provide a sign that deer are in the area.

God has left many telltale signs of His existence in the universe:

"Since the creation of the world God's invisible qualities—his eternal power and divine nature—have been clearly seen, being understood from what has been made, so that men are without excuse" (Romans 1:20).

In 2002 Ravi Zacharias told the United Nations about an illustration that his quantum physics professor at Cambridge University used. Dr. John Polkinghorne told his students that "if you were to analyze just one contingency" in the formation of the universe, the chances of everything coming into place in the correct way and time required would be "like taking aim at a one-square-inch object at the other end of the universe twenty billion light years away and hitting it bull's-eye."[1] In other words, there's no way this universe "just happened" to appear. It's a physical impossibility. The universe had to be created by a tremendously powerful and brilliant being.

Our explanations of the world's origins are similar to a grasshopper trying to figure out how a skyscraper came into being, but raised to the nth degree times infinity. Or as one person put it, it's like trying to explain the Internet to an ant. The chasm between an insect and us is nothing compared to the distance between God—the creator

Visit www.donnapartow.com and click Audios to learn more about "Signifying God." For practical help creating your personal card to signify God's care, visit www.donnapartow .com/care_cards.

and sustainer of the universe (Isaiah 40:12–13)—and our understanding of His thoughts, ideas, and abilities.

Psalm 19:1–2 says, "The heavens declare the glory of God; the skies proclaim the work of his hands. Day after day they pour forth speech." Speech? Do skies talk? Well, they certainly say something— they point to the presence of a creator. Scientists estimate that seventy

SIMPLE WAYS TO SHOW GOD'S CARE

- Buy a gently used blanket from a thrift store and donate it to a homeless shelter. Better yet, personally hand it to a homeless person.
- Give a homeless person a bottle of water.
- Sign up to be involved in an outreach-oriented ministry at your church.
- Give an extra tip to the waiter or waitress.
- Go through your closet, taking out anything you haven't worn in the last year and donate it to a charity thrift store.
- Choose your best outfit and donate it to a job-training program.
- Organize a neighborhood block party and get to know your neighbors.
- Take a coworker or neighbor out to lunch *just because*!

sextillion stars shine *within range of telescopes.*[2] This number does not include what exists beyond the view of telescopes. And not only has God created the skies, the Bible says He "calls [stars] each by name" (Isaiah 40:26).

The universe is a compelling sign that God exists, but it doesn't tell people what they really want to know: *Does God actually care*

- Donate books to your local school or library.
- Walk through your neighborhood picking up trash. Make it your goal to fill an entire trash bag.
- Bake cookies for your neighborhood fire or police department.
- Offer to help a neighbor with yard work or a household project.
- Next trash day, bring your neighbor's trash bin back from the curb.
- Go to a parking lot and wash car windows.
- Go to www.vistaprint.com and have a card created with a customized message such as: "This act of kindness brought to you by the God who created and cares for you." You could include your favorite Bible verse and, if you like, the name and location of the church you attend. Then, whenever God prompts you to demonstrate His care, you can leave behind a tangible footprint.[3]

about me as an individual? He may know the stars by name, but does He know my name? This is where we Christians are supposed to come in! It's not our responsibility to show forth God's power and brilliance; *it's our job to show His compassion.* And that's why even non-Christians sense something's wrong when we are hard, harsh, and judgmental. When Christianity is presented as nothing more than a list of rules and regulations, it doesn't sit right with people. It shouldn't sit right with us, either, because we are betraying the purpose for which God created us—He created us to be a sign that He cares about people.

A friend of mine was driving past a prostitute when he suddenly felt compelled to reach out to her. So he pulled over and called me. He walked up to the woman, spoke a few kind words to her, then handed her the phone and said, "Someone wants to talk with you." We chatted for a few minutes, and then I asked her, "When you woke up this morning, did you happen to say, 'God, if you're real, show me a sign'?" She began sobbing uncontrollably. "That's exactly what I said. How did you know?"

"Because God is real," I explained. "Who do you think told my friend to pull over in response to your prayer?"

This woman was astonished and overjoyed at the thought that the God of the universe cared enough about her to show her a sign in her hour of desperation. My friend and I were also amazed—amazed that God could use us in such a significant way simply because we took a few minutes to demonstrate that He exists and that He cares enough to comfort one hurting individual. But why should we have been so surprised? That's why we're here!

I proceeded to share with this woman how God sent His Son to pay the price for all her mistakes so that she could have a clean slate, a fresh start, right on the spot. She prayed with me—over the phone, standing there on her street corner—and invited the God of the universe to come into her heart and change her from the inside out. My friend stayed with this new believer while I made a phone call to the Salvation Army and made arrangements for her to get off the streets. The last I heard they were trying to get her into a job-placement program.

Every morning, all over the world, people wake up and say, "God, if You're real, show me a sign." God wants us so tuned in to Him that He can dial our number, so to speak, and say, "See that woman on aisle eight or that woman who just moved in down the street? She's looking for a sign that I care. Strike up a conversation with her. Invite her to church." He may even prompt you to offer practical help. When we listen and obey these inner promptings, we are letting our lives count. We are walking signs and wonders that point to God's existence. Talk about making a difference in this world!

My friend didn't set out that morning to make something happen. He wasn't trying to launch a national outreach to prostitutes; I don't think he's ever talked to one before or since. He simply allowed God to interrupt his day. He simply responded to God's prompting, gave up an hour of his time, and let God use him to make a significant impact upon this woman's life.

My friend Linda had a similar experience:

Last year, I took my kids on vacation to Walt Disney World in Florida. We were so exhausted from traveling that I overslept

and missed the first bus to the park. I was furious with myself.
My girlfriend told me to chill out in the room while she took
the kids to the hotel pool for an hour. When I walked into the
room, the maid was there. She was incredibly beautiful. Tall,
with long blond hair. But then I noticed such sadness in her
eyes. It broke my heart.

I struck up a conversation with her, and she just started
sobbing. She told me that she had gone to a modeling audi-
tion in Russia and that they had told her she was hired. She
couldn't believe her luck. But when she arrived in the United
States, she discovered that the modeling agency was a cover for
a prostitution ring. She was forced into working as a prostitute
at night and as a maid during the day.

I couldn't believe what I was hearing. It was like a scene
from a nightmarish movie. At that minute, I was so thankful
God let me oversleep. And I was so glad I decided to talk to
the maid instead of taking a nap as I had planned. I started
making phone calls. We found a ministry that helps these
women. Maybe it was dangerous, but we got her out of the
hotel within hours. The church was able to connect her with
Christians and with other Russian women who'd been through
the same ordeal.

You may be thinking, *Oh, I'll never encounter someone in such dire
straits.* But the truth is, every single day you pass by people who are
in desperate situations and need to know that God cares about their

predicaments. According to the Salvation Army, "It is estimated that nearly one million people are sold across international borders each year, having been bought and transported in slave-like conditions for sex and labor exploitation. The United States is one of the largest destination countries for trafficking victims from over fifty different countries."[4]

Linda did not wake up that morning with a mission to rescue someone. She was just trying to take her kids to Walt Disney World, but God had other plans for her. What plans might He have for you today? Could it be that God wants *you* to be the answer to someone's cry for help? Today, make a conscious effort to remain alert to those divine appointments God has prepared for you: at the grocery store, the nail salon, your workplace, your children's schools. Everywhere you go, God is at work, and He wants you to be part of it.

Every time you become part of an answered prayer, you are a sign to the world that God cares. Every time you show a small act of kindness and casually mention that you did it because God prompted you to, you are a sign to the world. Every kind word spoken in Jesus's name and every kind gesture done on His behalf become a trail of footprints upon the earth; proof positive that God not only exists but a sure sign that He is living in your neighborhood.

Several weeks after I thought I'd completed this chapter, I noticed a woman sitting on a street corner near my daughter's school. I decided that if she was still sitting there after I dropped off my daughter's lunch, I would know God wanted me to reach out. Sure enough, even though I was delayed at the school, the woman was still there.

The first thing I noticed was her thick African accent, so I asked her where she was from: Nigeria. (In this strife-torn country in West Africa, the average income is about $290 *a year*.[5]) I came right out and stated my purpose: "I believe God told me to check on you, to see if I could help you today." She immediately began crying. "I'm a Christian," she said. "I pray to God. Just when I think He forgets me, He always sends someone like you!" Her joy and relief were overwhelming as she shared one example after another of God's personal intervention. We alternated between crying and laughing, marveling at the goodness of God in bringing us together. If I hadn't forgotten to pack my daughter's lunch, I never would have met her!

Anna, who had taught art history at a Nigerian university, said she was brought here under false pretenses by someone who promised her a fabulous job in New York City in return for seven thousand dollars. Her extended family scraped the money together, believing that Anna would soon have enough money to provide for all of their needs. Instead, she discovered her papers were phony, and she was forced into illegal, manual labor for menial wages. Even so, she was only paid occasionally because those for whom she worked know that an illegal immigrant has no recourse. She had to take whatever they gave her, and sometimes they gave her nothing.

Fortunately, Anna had finally received a check for eight hundred dollars from the director of the senior care facility where she lives and works. She was sitting there, distraught, because no bank would cash it for her. She showed me the check, and I suggested we go to a branch of the credit union it was drawn against. We tracked down the nearest location, and, thankfully, they cashed the check. Then Anna declared excitedly that she could now afford to buy a phone card to call her family. We went to a store, where I surprised her by purchasing four phone cards, and she cried again.

This story isn't over yet. I just met Anna yesterday and am open to whatever else God may want me to do for her. But at the very least, my heart is filled with joy knowing that I was an answer to her prayer and proof positive that God does indeed live in this neighborhood.

He lives in your neighborhood, too. So be alert! And be prepared for God to disrupt your day. As we'll see in the next chapter, God has prepared good works for you to do.

Remember

You were created to be a sign to the world that God is real and that He cares. Open your heart to the possibility that *you* might be the answer to someone's prayer: *God, if You care, show me a sign.*

Reflect

Can you think of a time when someone was a sign to you that God cared? Can you think of a time when God used you to show His care to someone? Is there someone in your life right now who may need you to be a sign of God's care?

Reach

If possible, write a note to the person who served as a sign to you. Pray, asking God to lead you to one person to whom you can demonstrate God's care *today.*

Dear heavenly Father, I praise You for the masterwork of Your creation. For the sun, moon, and stars—for the beauty of everything that surrounds me. I can't imagine how anyone could behold Your creation and not acknowledge or appreciate You as the Creator. And yet I know it's true. So help me to be an unmistakable sign today. Holy Spirit, enable me to live my life today in such a way that I point people to You. Let me show someone that You care by taking the simple step of showing that I care. Open my spiritual eyes to at least one person to whom I can demonstrate Your care today. Amen.

7

God Has Prepared Good Works for You to Do

> For it is by grace you have been saved, through faith—
> and this not from yourselves, it is the gift of God—not by
> works, so that no one can boast. For we are God's work-
> manship, created in Christ Jesus to do good works, which
> God prepared in advance for us to do.
>
> EPHESIANS 2:8–10

In the previous chapter, I mentioned that Anna was sitting on a street corner. She had been there for at least twenty minutes when I picked her up. Surely at least a few Christians drove right past her that morning. Does that mean they're bad Christians? Did they ignore God when He told them to reach out to her? That's possible, but I actually believe God did *not* prompt anyone else. (Remember, He had before prompted other Christians concerning her, and they were clearly obedient.) God could easily have sent someone else who would have arrived before me, but I believe Anna was my assignment, my divine appointment.

God has assignments and divine appointments prepared for each of us every day. Just as we pray as we go, we must also serve along the way. What God has for *you* is unique and will reflect who you are and the life you live. A stay-at-home mom with a flexible schedule will receive different tasks than a business executive who rubs shoulders with influential people. Both are essential to the kingdom, and God has prepared good works for both, but the nature of those encounters will be very different.

Tammy has given birth seven times, so when she received a phone call from a twenty-four-year-old, unwed expectant mother, it was not difficult for her to imagine that serving as this woman's birthing coach was a good work God had prepared in advance for her to do. Tammy had never signed up to be someone's birthing coach; she had merely volunteered occasionally at the local crisis pregnancy center. God took it from there.

Of course, Tammy had to be willing to take the girl to the doctor and to invest time praying for her and getting to know her. She had to be willing to stay with this expectant mom through many hours of labor. Tammy says, "God has created a bond between us, and I am excited to see how I can mentor her [as a Christian] and in her role as a single mom."

Notice that Tammy isn't trying to run the entire crisis pregnancy center, but neither is she completely absorbed in herself and her own family. Instead, she simply put herself in the path of God's activity (by volunteering at the center) and opened her heart to the one young woman God sent. God prepared a strategic assignment for Tammy (with seven children underfoot) that suits both her life experience and the reality of her current situation.

The good works God has called you to do include your major roles and responsibilities: wife, businesswoman, mother, lawyer, Sunday-school teacher, friend, schoolteacher, and so on. Your spiritual gifts and natural abilities will often determine the types of opportunities God provides. Entire books have been devoted to discerning your place in the grand scheme of things based on such factors. I would strongly encourage you to explore and develop your gifts accordingly.

However, finding out what God is calling us to do is not strictly a big-picture thing. We tend to think only in terms of whether God is calling us to become the next Billy Graham, but God doesn't always give us the whole map. He often just gives us the "You are here" arrow. Most of the time, He only shows us where to put our foot next, often in the form of one thing we can do *today*. That could mean making a phone call to a hurting friend or digging in a sandbox with a child. It might mean praying for somebody God lays on your heart. It could mean leaving an encouraging note in your daughter's lunch bag or asking the checkout woman at Wal-Mart how she is.

How can you discover what God has prepared in advance for you to do? First, you can ask Him to show you what to do *today*. Be alert to divine appointments—those opportunities to speak a word of encouragement to the discouraged, to pray for the sick or hurting, to provide practical help to a friend, a neighbor or even a stranger in need.

Second, "Trust in the LORD with all your heart, and lean not on your own understanding [don't second-guess the big picture]; in all your ways acknowledge Him, and He shall direct your paths [so that your life will count]" (Proverbs 3:5–6, NKJV).

If this book sends Christians out into the world trying to concoct various schemes or to manufacture great things they can do for God, I will have done more harm than good. There is no prepackaged formula that we can *all* follow, because God has prepared works that are specifically suited to you. My husband serves as a great example. Within the past few months, he has brought city traffic to a halt on two occasions. The first time, he noticed a man in a wheelchair who couldn't catch an opportunity to cross a city street because cars were constantly turning, even on red lights. So he directed traffic to stop and walked the man across the street.

The second time, Jeff drove past an elderly woman whose trash can had fallen into a major street; she was dodging traffic trying to retrieve the strewn garbage. He made a U-turn, blocked traffic with his pickup truck, and cleaned the mess as the woman stood there in tears. After assisting her, he mentioned the church we attend, which was only a few blocks away.

As I shared these two stories with a gentleman as great examples of how we should *all* let our lives count, he looked at me earnestly and said, "I could never stop traffic like that. It would be dangerous."

For more insight into the good works God has prepared for you, take the free online "Assessment of Roles and Responsibilities." Visit www.donnapartow.com/roles.

I looked at him—he is maybe five foot seven and probably no more than a hundred and fifty pounds—and realized he was absolutely right! My husband is a giant of a man; that's why God taps *him* for assignments that require a large man who commands attention. But did you notice in the last chapter that Jeff did *not* pull over and assist the man who was offering free prayer?

God does not require everyone to stop traffic or pray for people by the side of the road. In fact, unlike other world religions, Christianity does not require specific activities to earn God's approval. Ephesians 2:8 asserts that we are saved by grace, not by doing good. Unfortunately, some Christians forget about verse 10, which explains what is supposed to come next, namely, doing the good works God prepared in advance for us. As the authors of *The Externally Focused Church* explain:

> Good news and accompanying good deeds are like two wings
> of an airplane.... Each gives "lift" to the other. To study the
> life and ministry of Jesus is to study a tapestry woven of good
> news and good deeds.... [His] good deeds paved the road over
> which his good news traveled.[1]

God intends us to live for His kingdom, not for ourselves. If we want to let our lives count, we must discover balance. We won't sit in the pew; nor will we run around like the proverbial chicken with her head cut off, trying to prove to God and the world that we are worth something. Instead we will ask Him to show us what He has prepared for us to do, and then we will do it.

We were designed to live for something larger than ourselves. We have been blessed to be a blessing, and deep inside, we *know it*. As we carry out those assignments that God has custom tailored for us, we will become truly alive, infused with joy and purpose. We not only let our lives count for the sake of the kingdom and for the sakes of others, but we also let our lives count for our own sakes because, as the old saying goes, "When I'm wrapped up in myself, I make a very small package!"

Many of the good works God has prepared for you can be accomplished outside the four walls of your church, so don't worry: you don't have to be a church insider to count.

Remember

God has assignments and divine appointments prepared for each of us every day. There is no prepackaged formula that we can *all* follow, because God has prepared works that are specifically suited to who you are and the life you live.

Reflect

What are some unique things about your lifestyle? What are your major roles and responsibilities? Can you think of opportunities you have had to serve that seemed customized to your life? Do you believe good deeds pave the road over which good news can travel? Can you think of experiences that give evidence to your belief?

Reach

Be alert to practical ways God might have you perform good deeds that might become the roads over which His good news can travel.

Dear heavenly Father, I thank You that I'm saved by grace. Forgive me for those times when I've trampled that grace underfoot by neglecting those good deeds You have prepared in advance for me. Forgive Your people for wanting to share the good news of the gospel without first being willing to perform those good deeds that would pave the way for a receptive hearing. Holy Spirit, help us to be more like Jesus, who not only taught the truth but also lived it by showing compassion to people in need. Lord, help me to pave a road or two today! Amen.

8

You Don't Have to Be a Church Insider to Count

Then the King will say to those on his right, "Come, you who are blessed by my Father; take your inheritance, the kingdom prepared for you since the creation of the world. For I was hungry and you gave me something to eat, I was thirsty and you gave me something to drink, I was a stranger and you invited me in, I needed clothes and you clothed me, I was sick and you looked after me, I was in prison and you came to visit me."… The King will reply, "I tell you the truth, whatever you did for one of the least of these brothers of mine, you did for me."

MATTHEW 25:34–36, 40

When I was in seventh grade, my next-door neighbor had a birthday party. She invited everyone in the class—except me. The party started during daylight, and I could hear the kids running around, boys chasing the girls, that kind of thing. I was hurt, but that was nothing compared to the hurt I felt when darkness fell, the

WORD OF THE WEEK

The Subject: God ordains certain men to hell on purpose

Isaiah 64:8 - *O Lord, thou art our Father; we are the clay; and thou our potter; and we all are the <u>work</u> of thy hand.*

> <u>work</u> - Hebrew: Maaseh-an action (good or bad); product; transaction; business

Romans 9:20-23 - *Who art thou that repliest against God? Shall the thing formed say to him that formed it, why hast thou made me thus? Hath not the potter the power over the clay of the same lump, to make one vessel unto honour and another unto dishonour -- What if God willing to show his wrath, and to make his power known, endured with much long suffering the vessels of wrath <u>fitted</u> to destruction: And that he might make known the riches of his glory on the vessels of mercy, which he hath afore prepared unto glory.*

> <u>fitted</u> - Greek: katartizo - to complete thoroughly; fit; frame; arrange; prepare. Thayer says this word speaks of men whose souls God has so constituted that they cannot escape destruction; <u>their mind is fixed that they frame themselves.</u>

Men get angry to think that we serve a God that can do as it pleases him. They actually think that an almighty God thinks the way they think and that he could not possibly form-fit a vessel to hell merely to show his wrath and power. Paul said he does. Men have difficulty perceiving a God that predestinates men (Rom. 8:29) on whom he desires to show his grace (unmerited favor) and mercy, that he may shower them throughout eternity with the riches of his glory. We like to believe that we must give him permission; if he is to operate in our hearts and minds. The Lord said, "My thoughts are not your thoughts, neither are your ways my ways. As the heavens are higher than the earth, so are my ways higher than your ways and my thoughts than your thoughts (Isaiah 55:8,9)". Our God is in the heavens: he hath done whatsoever he hath pleased (Psalms 115:3). He doeth whatsoever pleaseth him (Eccl 8:3). Thou, O Lord hast done as it pleased thee (Jonah 1:14). Whatsoever the Lord pleased, that did he in heaven, and earth, and in the seas, and in all deep places (Psalms 135:6). He does all his pleasure (Isa. 46:10; Isa. 44:24-28; Eph. 1:5,9; Philippians 2:13). It is Jesus that holds the keys to death and hell (Rev. 1:18), not Satan. God will intentionally cast these evil vessels of wrath into hell and lock them up for eternity because it is not his pleasure to draw them to him (John 6:44). This doctrine angers men, though it is taught throughout the pages of God's Holy Book. Men do not have a Biblical view of the living God when they think he is not in control of all things including the minds and hearts of all men. God is not only love to the vessels of mercy, but he is a consuming fire (Deut 4:24) upon the vessels of wrath fitted to destruction. We do not serve a God who is Superman that can only shake mountains, implode blackholes, and explode quasars. The God of the universe can harden and soften the hearts of men at will (Rom 9:18; Ezek. 36:26). He giveth not account of any of his matters (Job 33:13).

GRACE AND TRUTH MINISTRIES

P.O. Box 1109 Hendersonville, TN 37077
Jim Brown - Bible Teacher • 824-8502

Radio Broadcast – Sat. Morn. 8am 1300 AM Dial WNQM
TV – Mon. & Sat 10pm, Wed. & Fri. 12am Channel 176;
Tues. & Thurs. 5pm Channel 3; Thurs. 11am Channel 49

Join us for fellowship at 394 West Main Street on
Sunday Mornings @ 11:00am, Sunday Evenings @ 7:00pm,
Wednesday Evenings @ 7:00pm
Or
Watch us live via U-Stream on the web at
www.graceandtruth.net

boys left, and the girls moved to the bedroom for a slumber party. My neighbor's bedroom window was directly across from my bedroom, maybe twenty feet away. It was a spring night, and the bedroom windows were open. I turned out all the lights in my bedroom and pressed my nose against the window screen. Tears streamed down my face as I watched my classmates' every move shining out through the darkness. It was almost like being at a drive-in movie theater, except I didn't have any popcorn.

A few months later, I decided to take revenge on the neighbor by inviting everyone in the class but her to a swimming party. The morning of the party, I had a saxophone lesson, and as I walked home, dragging the heavy instrument case behind me, my heart was heavy too. I knew the idea was cruel, but I told myself that she'd done it to me first. I pushed sympathy aside and got busy setting up in the backyard. I covered a little table with a paper cloth and set out some pretzels and potato chips and soda. Then I sat down to wait for the party to begin.

It never did. No one came. *No one,* and I ended up feeling even more alone.

I wonder if you can relate to that feeling—the feeling of being on the outside looking in, the feeling that there's a party going on and everyone has been invited to it, except for you. Maybe you show up at church, week after week, but you feel like you're on the outside looking in. Everyone else seems to count, but you count for nothing.

I used to sit in church, racking my brains and beating myself over the head, because no matter how hard I tried, I could not see the world through the rose-colored glasses everyone else seemed to have been born wearing. No matter how many books I read, no matter how many classes I took, I still couldn't get my act together. I couldn't make it through a week without some catastrophe. Even now, after twenty-five years as a Christian, I am still not a church insider. Sometimes I still feel like I'm on the outside looking in.

However, I've discovered that you don't have to be a church insider to let your life count. Plenty of people in this world, especially in this country, long to know God better, and many are even Christians, but they will never attend church. I know because I meet them all the time in coffee shops, airports, and taxicabs. So don't limit your thinking. Don't immediately think that letting your life count *only* means doing some kind of ministry at your church.

Let me give you some examples of women who are letting their lives count in unconventional ways.

If Geri walked into some churches, they'd either ask her to leave or make her feel so unwelcome she wouldn't want to come back. Geri is a biker, and she looks like one: leather, tattoos, body piercings—the

For up-to-date information on ministry opportunities outside your church, including outreaches sponsored by Donna Partow Ministries, visit www.donnapartow.com/opportunities. If your church would like to host a Let Your Life Count conference, designed to motivate church attendees to live outreach as a lifestyle, please e-mail lylc@donnapartow.com for details.

whole deal. She spends her time in biker bars and has a special place in her heart for barmaids because she used to be one.

Several years ago, she persuaded a small group of them to come to work (yes, at the bar) forty-five minutes early so they could discuss my book *Becoming a Vessel God Can Use*. These women wanted to know how they could be used by God, in spite of their professions. They wanted to know if they could still let their lives count; Geri gave them hope that they could.

Another woman I know, Jane, who is in her late sixties, didn't think she had any special talent that would count for the kingdom. She had "never done anything but raise babies." She has attended church all her life, but she's never taught women's Bible study, and, truth be told, she has never attended one either. "That crowd is so gossipy," she explained to me. "I don't care for that."

Then a few years ago, a friend told her about the need for people to rock babies, especially crack babies, whose drug-addicted mothers had either abandoned them or had their hands full fighting for their own recoveries. Jane immediately felt led to volunteer to hold babies at the local children's hospital, and now twice a week she sits in a rocking chair in the children's ward singing "Jesus Loves Me" and "The B-I-B-L-E" to babies in need of love and touch. Jane's not a church insider and doesn't want to be, but she prays day and night that the babies she comforts will some day find their places in Christ.

Perhaps you have never been and never will be a church insider. That's okay. A great big world is out there that holds unlimited possibilities to let your life count. One of my favorite organizations to work with is the Salvation Army. Believe me, you don't have to be a church insider to assist with their ministries. Opportunities to serve range from gathering and organizing donated clothing to serving in soup kitchens, visiting prisoners, cleaning up after natural disasters, comforting battered women and their frightened children, wrapping Christmas gifts, and of course, standing on street corners ringing bells during the holiday season! Few of these ministries require special talents; none requires you to walk through church doors; all require a willingness to let your life count.

The world needs fewer church insiders and more church outsiders, that is, people who are willing to go *outside* the church walls to let their lives count in the community. Word of Grace Church sets aside the entire month of November as Heart for Others month. It's a time for the congregation to look beyond the church walls—something too few churches in America do enough of. The senior minister, Dr. Gary Kinnaman, developed the idea nearly a decade ago as a practical way to help church members look outward. He recalls, "I saw a gap between church work at one extreme and foreign missions on the other. Conservative churches traditionally have invested millions in overseas ministry but, at times, have done very little about needs down the street. I also felt that getting people connected locally would in time open their hearts to others in cross-cultural settings. Studies have shown that many Americans, especially the younger generation, wonder why we would be concerned about people in, let's say, Uganda, when there are underprivileged and homeless people around the corner. We start locally but stretch people globally."

REACHING CHURCH OUTSIDERS

The following ministries target those outside the church. Find out how you can get involved today. (This information provided here was quoted or adapted from the Web sites at press time. For updated information, please visit the applicable site.)

Compassion International: www.compassion.com
"Compassion International exists as an advocate for children, releasing them from spiritual, economic, social, and physical poverty and enabling them to become responsible, fulfilled Christian adults. Founded by the Reverend Everett Swanson in 1952, Compassion began providing Korean War orphans with food, shelter, education, and health care, as well as Christian training. Today, Compassion helps more than seven hundred thousand children in more than twenty countries." If you would like to sponsor a child for a small monthly donation, visit their Web site.

Habitat for Humanity: www.habitat.org
Habitat for Humanity International is a nonprofit, nondenominational Christian housing organization that builds

(continued on the next page)

simple, decent, affordable houses in partnership with those who lack adequate shelter. Since 1976, Habitat has built more than one hundred seventy-five thousand houses, providing shelter for nearly nine hundred thousand people worldwide. According to *Habitat World,* the publication for Habitat for Humanity International, "A new Habitat house is being built, on average, every twenty-six minutes as Habitat for Humanity builds thousands of houses across the United States and in more than eighty other countries.… By the end of 2005, Habitat expects to have completed two hundred thousand houses for a million people." To get involved locally, visit their Web site and type in your ZIP code. Other options including using your vacation to build homes overseas. (Your church might explore building an entire village in a third-world country!)

Salvation Army: www.salvationarmyusa.org
"Salvation Army social service programs meet the basic needs of daily life for those without the resources to do so themselves. Often, the programs provide food, shelter, clothing, financial assistance to pay utilities, and other necessities. Whether it is financial planning and job placement for a young, single mother living in a Salvation Army transitional facility; health care and residential assistance for a family

dealing with illness; or counseling and advocacy for a victim of spousal abuse, the Salvation Army is with those it serves every step of the way. They operate 120 Adult Rehabilitation Centers, where men and women receive the care they need to overcome the struggles of addiction to drugs and alcohol.

"The Red Kettles and bell ringers are perhaps the most visible community-wide Salvation Army program. The nickels, dimes, and dollars put into the kettles provide needy families with Thanksgiving and Christmas dinners, gifts for children, coats and shoes for kids with none to wear, and visitation to the elderly and imprisoned who have no one to care for them."

Samaritan's Purse: www.samaritanspurse.org
Founded by Franklin Graham, "Samaritan's Purse is a nondenominational evangelical Christian organization providing spiritual and physical aid to hurting people around the world. Since 1970, Samaritan's Purse has helped meet needs of people who are victims of war, poverty, natural disasters, disease, and famine with the purpose of sharing God's love through His Son, Jesus Christ." According to their Web site, "Our emergency relief programs provide desperately needed assistance to victims of natural disaster, war, disease, and famine. As we

(continued on the next page)

offer food, water, and temporary shelter, we meet critical needs and give people a chance to rebuild their lives.

"Our community development and vocational programs in impoverished villages and neighborhoods help people break the cycle of poverty and give them hope for a better tomorrow.

"We impact the lives of vulnerable children through educational, feeding, clothing, and shelter programs that let them know they are not forgotten.

"We provide first-class treatment in the Name of the Great Physician through our medical projects, as well as supplying mission hospitals with much needed equipment and supplies."

One way to get involved (as a church or individual) is through Operation Christmas Child. "Operation Christmas Child brings joy and hope to children in desperate situations around the world through gift-filled shoe boxes and the Good News of God's love. This program of Samaritan's Purse provides an opportunity for people of all ages to be involved in a simple, hands-on mission project while focusing on the true meaning of Christmas—Jesus Christ, God's greatest gift. Along with shoe-box gifts, millions of children are given gospel booklets in their own languages. In 2004, [Operation Christmas Child] collected over seven million shoe-box gifts worldwide and distributed them to children in ninety-five countries."

World Vision: www.worldvision.org
"World Vision is a Christian relief and development organization dedicated to helping children and their communities worldwide reach their full potential by tackling the causes of poverty." They provide annual assistance to "more than eighty-five million people in nearly one hundred countries, including the United States." Perhaps best known for their child sponsorship program, World Vision "helps people discover and use their own visions, skills, and resources to move from abject poverty to abundant living. They target critical needs: clean water, reliable food supplies, access to basic health care, education, and income-generating microeconomic development." World Vision also "responds to sudden natural disasters and slow-building humanitarian emergencies around the world. [Their goal] is to save lives and reduce suffering by tracking crises, prepositioning emergency supplies for immediate response, and remaining after the crisis to rebuild and restore communities." World Vision offers a wide variety of involvement opportunities—both in the United States and around the world—for individuals, youth groups, and churches. To sponsor a child, call (888) 511-6592.

Even though he's the pastor of a five-thousand-member congregation, Dr. Kinnaman routinely spends time outside the church walls, volunteering his time at a nearby food bank. "I've done this," he says, "because it's so easy for pastors to get lost in the maze of their own church. Volunteering in the community gives me a vastly different view of what so many people are facing, and it allows me to be an example to the people in our church. You know, if Pastor Gary can do it, they can, too!"

If you feel like an outsider in church, why not contact a charity or relief organization in your area to find out how you and your family might get involved? If you are a church insider, why not use your influence to encourage your church to begin looking outside its own four walls? Don't wait until you feel good enough to get involved.

Remember

You don't have to be a church insider to let your life count. Many people outside the church walls need to see the love of God.

Reflect

Are you a church insider? Have you made others feel like outsiders? If you are not a church insider, think of other places in your community where you might let your life count.

If you are active in a local church, look around next Sunday. Ask God to reveal to you one woman who feels like she's on the outside looking in. Make it a point to strike up a conversation with her. Invite her to the party! In fact, you can invite her to your next outreach adventure that takes *you* outside the church!

Dear heavenly Father, I thank You that I don't have to be a church insider to count. I pray, right now, for the countless souls who will never walk through church doors—especially if no one ever invites them. Open my heart, and open the hearts of those in authority at my home church, to the tremendous needs that exist outside the four walls of our building. At the same time, open my eyes to see those within my church who feel like outsiders. Show me how I can make them feel welcome in Jesus's name. Amen.

9

Don't Wait Until You Feel Good Enough

Not that I have already obtained all this, or have already
been made perfect, but I press on to take hold of that for
which Christ Jesus took hold of me.

PHILIPPIANS 3:12

*G*od called me into ministry in July 1980, the day after I prayed
to surrender my life to Him. He told me: *I'm going to take you
to retreat centers just like this one, all over the world, and I'm going to use
you in a mighty way for My kingdom.*

Although God didn't specify *how* my life would count, I knew
instinctively I'd never be a camp nurse or a cook or a counselor or a
song leader. I just assumed I'd be the one doing the talking because
my mother had been calling me Mouth Almighty for as long as I
could remember. Yes, indeed, I was the mouth that roared. My mom
swore you could hear my "whisper" from a mile away; my sister can
verify this, because we shared a bed growing up, and many a night it
was my so-called whispering that got us both in trouble.

So there was no doubt in my mind that God wanted me to speak publicly about Him some day. But "some day" turned out to be a much longer wait than I had imagined! I spent more than fifteen years dreaming of the day when I would finally be good enough to speak in Christian circles. I'll never forget the first time I went to hear a famous Christian author (who shall remain nameless). I listened in absolute awe. The Proverbs 31 woman had come to life before my very eyes: everything about her life seemed perfect, from her morning devotions and personal grooming to her marriage, family, and finances. When the conference was over, I walked out that door thinking, *What an amazing woman. I could never be like her.*

I had registered for that conference looking for encouragement, but left feeling discouraged instead. It took me nearly two decades to get the revelation: few people ever feel good enough to serve God. And the people who think they're good enough are either in denial or seriously scary. Maybe you tell yourself, *I'll take that spiritual gifts class, that parenting class, three more months in counseling. I'll read one more book on prayer, and then I'll be good enough.* But no matter how hard you try to be a good parent, friend, employee, or Christian, something inside always tells you, *Not good enough.*

No one has ever been good enough. I'm not! If you're not either, know that we're in good company. The apostle Paul himself said,

> Not that I have already obtained all this, or have already
> been made perfect, but I press on to take hold of that for
> which Christ Jesus took hold of me. Brothers, I do not con-
> sider myself yet to have taken hold of it. But one thing I do:

Forgetting what is behind and straining toward what is ahead,
I press on toward the goal to win the prize for which God has
called me heavenward in Christ Jesus. (Philippians 3:12–14)

Throughout his ministry Paul denounced people who used the
Old Testament to discourage and de-motivate people by telling them
they weren't good enough. Yet some people take these verses and use
them for the same purpose. I've had Christians tell me, "Paul said forget what's behind. You're supposed to forget all that junk in your past.
What's wrong with you? Snap out of it!" These people have forgotten
that we're supposed to use the Bible as a sword to defeat the forces of
darkness, not as a weapon to beat other people down.

Unlike me, Paul wasn't trying to forget that he'd been a drug addict,
floozy, or some kind of loser that everyone looked down on. To the con-
trary, he had lived his life trying to be perfect, and he'd come close. He
had everything going for him—great family, premium education, a
prestigious position (Philippians 3:4–6). The guy had the credentials
that counted. And he says, as far as "legalistic righteousness"—that is,
always doing exactly the right thing—he was "faultless."

But it did him no good. The Bible clearly says, "If righteousness
could be gained through the law, Christ died for nothing" (Galatians
2:21). That's what Paul is talking about here when he says, "I'm forgetting what's behind." Look at the context. He's not talking about
forgetting his mistakes. He was forgetting that whole trip of trying to
prove to himself and God and the planet that somehow he could be
good enough. He realized that striving to reach such a goal was like
walking in circles.

You may be thinking, *Not* feeling *good enough is one thing, but my problem isn't just a feeling, it's a fact. I lack the right qualifications.* If so, know this. Your lack of qualifications may be the very thing that makes you *most* qualified to let your life count in the real world, where ordinary people live. No one doubts that the pastor of a megachurch or a counselor with a PhD in psychology can live a life that counts. What the world needs to see is that regular people, those who lack impressive credentials, can count as well. After all, how many of us will ever teach at Harvard or Yale or stand in the pulpit in front of thousands of people? Not very many.

This message is not just for those like me who have an unseemly past. It's also for people who were raised in the church, who've lived upright, godly lives, but no matter what they do, something inside always says, *Not quite there yet.* I meet people all the time who've been in church for thirty years who still don't feel good enough to teach the Bible. Yet an African preacher I know says, "In my country, if you've been a Christian for three years, we make you a pastor!"

The Bible doesn't say serve God only if you feel qualified, if your kids turned out perfectly and your husband worships the ground you walk on. It commands older women to "train the younger women" (Titus 2:3–5). It doesn't say, "If you have lots of self-confidence and

---

For more on this subject, listen online to "I'm Not Good Enough Either!" Visit www.donnapartow.com and click Audios.

spare time." It says, "Train them." It doesn't say you need to grab a microphone or even form a small group; actually, the type of training referenced here is best done one on one in the privacy of a home. Every Christian has someone who's younger, both in age and in faith. If you became a Christian an hour ago, you're spiritually older than the person who's not yet a Christian. You don't need to attend seminary to tell someone what God has done in your life.

People are dying and going to hell while we obsess over whether we're good enough to tell them Jesus lived a perfect life and paid the price for them to go to heaven because He knew not one of us would ever be good enough. What are we thinking? Listen, if I were trapped in a burning building, I wouldn't care whether or not the guy who rescued me had a perfect family or a degree in theology. I'd just be thankful to be alive.

The biggest lie the Enemy has perpetrated in the contemporary church is that our lives won't count until we get our acts together, that our lives won't count until we can say, "Well, a long, long time ago I used to have problems, but ever since I met Jesus all my problems have miraculously disappeared and I've been transformed into Barbie with a Bible." He wants us to believe that until then, we better keep our mouths shut and not tell a soul anything about our faith. Until then, we don't have anything to offer, so it's better to just sit in the pew, taking up space.

Don't get me wrong. Obviously, we should cooperate with God as He slowly transforms us from the inside out. It's been aptly said that God meets us where we are but loves us too much to leave us there. He wants us to make forward progress. But while we're cooperating with God to transform our own lives, He wants us actively involved in transforming the lives of others. In fact, the process of helping others is often the very tool God will use to move us closer and closer to the people we long to be.

Isn't it interesting that when God halted Paul on the Damascus road, He told him, "Now get up and go into the city, and you will be told what you must do" (Acts 9:6)? That's because God knew what Paul was like! What a perfectionist he was! So He specifically commanded him, "Don't wait until you think you're ready—do it *now*! Get up *now*!" Paul had been a Christian for about a nanosecond. Do you think he felt qualified to preach the gospel? Of course not! But God said, in essence, "Just go where I send you, and I'll tell you what to do when you get there."

This is the same message Jesus told my friend Sandy, which is why she didn't fall for the lie that she had to wait a long, long time to be good enough to help others. She recalls:

At forty years of age, I had many personal decisions to regret, and the idea of forgiveness seemed far from possible. One day, while standing in the shower, I cried out to God and wrote in the steam on the glass door "God, help me." He said, *Okay, but we'll do it My way.*

Not long after crying out to God in the shower, I walked through the door of a local sanctuary and sat alone in the back pew. I reached for the church bulletin to avoid small talk and eye contact. There in the small print I found a two-sentence request for people who might be interested in traveling to the

Dominican Republic to help a Christian organization build a school for children in a Third World village. My heart began to pound, and my hands began to sweat. I didn't even know where the island was located; how could I possibly be so excited?

Sandy had no idea what she was getting herself into—she wasn't even a Christian yet—but she registered anyway! That was six years ago. She became a believer on her first mission trip and has been on four more since then. Sandy didn't wait until she felt qualified; she just responded to the prompting of God.

Will you make a decision, right now, that you will never again use *not good enough* as an excuse to sit on the sidelines? The God who sends you is the God who is great enough to sustain you. But as you go, remember to walk in humility.

Remember

Very few people ever feel good enough to serve God, and those who do are self-deceived. Even the apostle Paul acknowledged that he hadn't arrived spiritually, but he was pressing on. We should do likewise.

Reflect

Think of a time when you refused to reach out or get involved because you didn't think you were good enough. In what ways do you see the cause of Christ being hindered because people are waiting to *feel* good enough? How would the church (and the world) be different if *everyone* was willing to be used by God, whether or not they considered themselves good enough?

Reach

Think of a Christian in your circle of influence who is uninvolved (other than attending church). Look for an opportunity to explore this issue of not feeling good enough to determine if *that* is what's holding him or her back. Then tell that person what God has shown you concerning this issue. You might take a step further and offer to jump into ministry together, agreeing that even though neither of you is good enough, God is great enough to work through your lives anyway.

Dear heavenly Father, I acknowledge that I am not now, nor will I ever become, good enough to serve a perfect, holy God. Forgive me for every opportunity I've allowed to pass by because I just didn't think I was good enough to let my life count. Thank You for the example of the apostle Paul, who was willing to admit his weaknesses and press on at the same time. Holy Spirit, empower me to press on. Open my eyes to those around me who are being held back from letting their lives count because they don't feel good enough, either. Empower us to move forward in faith, believing that You are great enough to work through us. Amen.

10

Walk in Humility

> Humble yourselves [feeling very insignificant] in the pres-
> ence of the Lord, and He will exalt you [He will lift you
> up and make your lives significant].
>
> JAMES 4:10, AMP

*N*ow that I've pointed out that you're as good enough as the
rest of us to let your life count, I need to add a word of
warning. Sometimes as we begin to let our lives count, especially in
ways that appear significant to those around us, we can become vulnerable to pride. Even those who start from humble beginnings need
to remain on guard because the Bible warns us, "Prides goes before
destruction, a haughty spirit before a fall" (Proverbs 16:18) and "Before
his downfall a man's heart is proud, but humility comes before honor"
(Proverbs 18:12).

We see this clearly in the life of Peter, who was working in the not
very prestigious field of fishing when Jesus said to him and his
brother, "Come, follow me" and "at once they left their nets and followed him" (see Matthew 4:18–20). Did you ever wonder why Peter

and the others followed Jesus so quickly? Was Jesus walking around in slow motion with a halo hovering over his head, as He's sometimes portrayed in old movies? Were the disciples inexplicably following after Him like hypnotized zombies? Was it really a giant leap of faith, as most of us have been taught?

No.

The disciples followed Jesus for a very practical reason. In Jesus's day, every Jewish boy had the goal of becoming a rabbi, because that's who counted most in their society. Jewish boys began studying in Hebrew school at age five. In the first level of education, they had to memorize the first five books of the Bible. Those who succeeded were considered smart enough and good enough to be promoted to the next level, where they memorized the entire Old Testament. If they were smart enough and good enough, they then went on to the third level, where they studied and memorized a mountain of rabbinical teachings. Those who made it that far had only one more step on the journey toward becoming a rabbi. A rabbi had to invite them to be his disciples. It was up to the individual rabbis to hand-select those students whom they felt were good enough to follow them, to learn their teachings. But these rabbis didn't just teach their students in a school setting. These disciples actually lived with the rabbis and followed them everywhere they went.

So we can assume that Peter's job as a fisherman was, to a certain degree, a badge of shame. Either he hadn't measured up or none of the rabbis had seen any great religious potential in him. (Maybe they had heard him put his foot in his mouth a time or two and decided there was no way he was ever going to be a spiritual leader!) Jesus's invitation presented Peter with a choice—remaining a fisherman or becoming a rabbi's disciple. The choice was a no-brainer.

Wouldn't you have done the same? Think about it. Let's say you were working the night shift in a factory or serving breakfast at the Waffle House, and the president of the United States walked in and said, "Come, follow me, and I'll make you ambassador to the Bahamas." How long do you think it would take you to make the decision?

Perhaps you can relate to Peter. You feel like you haven't made the grade in religious circles or that no one seems to think you have much spiritual or leadership potential. Perhaps you almost skipped this chapter because you've never accomplished anything you're especially proud of. Be careful. Peter went from "no-account" fisherman to one of the Twelve, and it went right to his head.

Peter didn't just sit passively in a church pew and watch Jesus minister. Jesus sent out the aspiring rabbis, including Peter, to heal the sick, raise the dead, drive out demons—in other words, to do what they had watched Jesus do (see Matthew 10:1–8). Apparently, Peter was very effective. If he had botched it, if he had created some catastrophe, at least one of the gospel writers probably would have mentioned it. So Peter assumed he was on the way to the top. Then, Jesus chose him to be one of the three disciples to go with Him to the literal mountaintop, where Jesus was transfigured into all His heavenly radiance, and Moses and Elijah appeared (see Matthew 17:1–9). That must have cinched it for Peter. He must have been thinking: *This is my future! Jesus is my mentor, and I'm going to become just like Him.* Of course, the thought of becoming like Jesus through crucifixion was the furthest thing from Peter's mind. He thought a life that counts is a life that's exalted; he didn't understand that a life that counts is characterized by humble service.

Sometimes the higher we go—especially if we get there in a hurry—the harder we fall. Such was the case with Peter. After such an awesome start, he fell on his face. Just hours after vowing to follow Jesus to His death, Peter denied ever having known Him (see Matthew 26:69–75). Peter wasn't a coward. Earlier that same evening, he had pulled out his sword and been willing to fight to protect his hopes of becoming a powerful rabbi when Jesus was crowned king in Jerusalem. Peter was willing to fight for respect in the religious community, for the opportunity to be honored in social circles. When following Christ meant earthly success, Peter was right there. But when it meant suffering and the death of his dreams, he balked. He was disillusioned, perhaps fearing that the last three years of his life—indeed all the years he'd studied to become a rabbi—had been a waste.

Peter fell because of pride. He was worried about how others might perceive him. If we're not careful, we'll fall into the same trap. Since we all long for significance, we are thrilled when we sense God saying, "Come, follow Me." We believe it's the start of something great. Then we become disillusioned when people don't treat us like we're someone special, when we don't receive the status we were secretly hoping for. We want to run away when God starts teaching us the painful lesson of humility.

Unfortunately, humility is almost always the fruit of brokenness, and no one enjoys the process. I met Mike Wolff while teaching at a writers' conference and immediately connected with the journey God was taking him through. In fact, I nicknamed him Peter. For twenty-five years, Mike had tried to live a model Christian life. He had actively served his church, leading worship and teaching Bible studies, while building a highly successful real estate career. Then the bottom began to fall out for no apparent reason. Real estate sales that typically fell together fell through instead. Once a leader in his church, he suddenly found himself at odds with the leadership, and he bowed out of his various commitments. His promising writing career came to a screeching halt, and one of his children suddenly began manifesting serious problems. He recalls, "I wasn't doing anything differently than I had ever done before, and yet life was literally crumbling all around me." It made no sense.

Eventually, Mike camped out in the Rocky Mountains where he fasted for three days, determined to find some answers. Already a broken man, he cried out to God, "Break me, Lord. Whatever it takes, make me the man You want me to be." He sensed God speaking to his heart and came down off the mountain, hoping his desperate pleas would bring an end to the trials. Instead, life got even worse. Mike turned to the book of Job and the life of David for answers. He began meditating on the Psalms. He recalls, "I found in them a man I could

To hear "Called and Commissioned," a complete message on the life of Peter, visit www.donnapartow.com and click Audios.

truly relate to: one who had been promised the reign of all Israel and yet found himself hiding in caves, afraid for his own life. He knew how to walk through the valley of the shadow of death."

Through the life of Job, Mike realized that "there is a humbling, a breaking that God institutes in our lives and calls us into. As His Spirit can take us to heights we could never attain by our own means, He can also take us to depths that defy description in an effort to break us of our pride." That's what God is after: the insidious sin of pride. And He loves us enough to stop at nothing to deal the death-blow to it. As Mike discovered, "The more good we think we are doing, the greater the risk. Satan has traps set all along the way, land mines for the newest of babes and the grayest of seasoned travelers, and he knows pride is the trap to set for the latter."

One way or another, anyone who desires to serve God must be humbled. Either we choose to humble ourselves, or God will do it for us. We can cultivate humility by reminding ourselves daily that we can do nothing to make our lives count for eternity. Anything of any value that's accomplished through our lives is solely the work of God and because of His infinite mercy.

But please don't confuse humility with self-loathing, which means beating yourself up. And don't confuse it with low self-esteem, either. Humility isn't thinking less of yourself; it's *thinking of yourself less.* It's not putting yourself down; it's putting the needs of others ahead of your personal agenda. In fact, anytime you are talking about your-self—even if only to put yourself down—you are not operating in humility. That's pride masquerading as false humility.

When we understand true humility, we understand that it's not about us. It's all about God. This is a tremendously freeing realization, because we understand that we have nothing to prove and nothing to hide. Few books have had a greater impact on my life than Andrew Murray's *Humility.* In it, he observes: "The seemingly insignificant acts of daily life are the tests of eternity.... It is in our most unguarded moments that we truly show who we are and what we are made of."[1] Who are you in those unguarded moments when no one else sees you? Do you think of yourself as better than others? Do you think of yourself as worse than others? Either way, you are not walking in humility. The truly humble person walks with absolute confidence, knowing that she is simply an empty vessel through whom God wants to accomplish His work.

If we fail to walk in humility, pride will taint our endeavors and haunt our steps, perhaps taking us down just when we think we are standing the tallest. One giant fall can leave devastation in its wake; just ask any pastor who fell into sexual sin or financial scandal because he thought more of himself than of the needs of the people. Jesus never put Himself above anyone else; instead, He washed the disciples' feet and laid down His life for us all.

Peter apparently learned the lesson of humility, which is why he urges us: "All of you, clothe yourselves with humility toward one another, because, 'God opposes the proud but gives grace to the humble.' Humble yourselves, therefore, under God's mighty hand, that he may lift you up in due time" (1 Peter 5:5–6). We clothe ourselves in humility by choosing daily to confess our sins readily and by coming into close relationship with a handful of believers to whom we've granted permission to call us on it when we start to get a bit full of ourselves.

The surest path to humility is allowing God to strip us of all motives other than one: letting Christ's love compel us. When we do things for any other reason, we are opening the doorway to pride.

Remember

Pride is a very real potential pitfall for everyone who wants to let her life count, and that's why it's important to cultivate humility. But humility doesn't mean thinking less of yourself; it means thinking of yourself less.

Reflect

What percentage of your waking hours do you spend thinking about the needs of others? What percentage do you spend thinking about yourself? What does that indicate about your level of humility?

Reach

Make it a point to treat someone, perhaps even a total stranger, as more important than yourself today. For example, even if you are in a hurry, deliberately let someone go in front of you in line at the grocery store. When you evaluate ministry opportunities, give extra consideration to those that will *not* draw special attention to you.

Dear heavenly Father, I acknowledge that I've stumbled into the pitfall of pride many times. Even as I've taken this journey to letting my life count, there have been moments when I've felt tempted to pat myself on the back. Forgive me, too, for the self-loathing that's really just pride masquerading as humility. Lord, I don't want to think less of myself; I want to think of myself less. Holy Spirit, open my eyes to those anonymous or low-profile opportunities to serve that won't feed my ego. Today, I desire to clothe myself in humility by making a conscious effort to treat others as more important than myself. Show me opportunities to do that as I journey through the day. Amen.

11

Let Christ's Love Compel You

If you love me, you will obey what I command.

JOHN 14:15

If you've read any of my previous writings,[1] you know that I was a promiscuous drug dealer before I became a Christian. I won't rehash all of that here, except to say that when God miraculously set me free from drugs, I wanted to prove to Him that He'd never be sorry for choosing me. I had been a bad girl; now I was going to show Him and the world what a good girl I could be. My church told me what to do to become a model Christian and to keep God happy, starting with trading in my string bikini for a one-piece bathing suit. They even gave me checklists and charts to keep track of all I was supposed to do.

Over time, my desire to obey God degenerated into a sense of duty. My dry brand of legalistic Christianity was nothing more than a set of beliefs and a list of dos and don'ts. I thought I could make my life count if I obeyed Paul's admonishment to "watch [my] life and doctrine closely" (1 Timothy 4:16). If I did this, then God would be pleased with me, people would be impressed with me, and my life would count for something. Instead I turned into a sanctimonious jerk whose underlying motive for obedience was pride.

I was so proud of my Bible knowledge, so proud of all the verses I had highlighted, underlined, and asterisked, which I mostly did so people around me would *notice* that when the pastor said "turn to passage such and so," I already had it covered. I was so proud of my good doctrine. So proud of my politics. So proud that I was a home-schooling mother. While there is nothing wrong with many of these things, I was doing them for all the wrong reasons.

So, not surprisingly, I burned out—just like many people who do good things out of a sense of duty. We burn out or dry up. Let's be honest enough to admit that there are lots of dry bones in them thar pews! We all know people like this. Not only is there no *life* in their Christian life, they drain the life out of everyone around them.

Eventually, my burnout degenerated into an attitude that said, "Why bother? This Christianity trip doesn't work, and frankly, I don't care anymore." My soul couldn't survive the doctrine-driven life. My church had so emphasized obedience for self-congratulation's sake that I never knew there was another reason to obey! Then I met a pastor who introduced me to the concept of sowing and reaping. He explained that we should obey God because every choice we make directly affects the quality of our lives. Throughout Scripture, God presents if-then scenarios. He says *if* we do such and such, *then* the results will be such and such.

Unfortunately, I then exchanged the doctrine-driven life for the formula-driven life. I tithed so that God would give me more money. I followed a particular parenting program so my kids would be guaranteed to turn out perfectly. I decided to do *this specific thing* in order to get *that specific result.*

I call this approach to faith Mechanistic Christianity. When we embrace this brand of Christianity, *get* becomes the operative word in our theology and life. We obey God in order to *get* His blessings. When we obey in order to *get,* we reduce God to Our Vending Machine which Art in Heaven. If we don't *get* exactly what we bargained for, we *get* disillusioned and walk away. That's what happened to me.

I suspect that some people reading this book may obey God merely out of a sense of duty. Maybe even you. Perhaps you are in the burned-out or dried-up phase. Or maybe you've been obeying God, hoping to get something specific in return, and now doubt and disillusionment are creeping in. Don't get me wrong, obeying God out of a sense of duty—doing what's right simply because it's the right thing to do—is certainly better than disobedience. Obeying because you understand God's principles of sowing and reaping, and because you believe God is true to His word, is even better, as long as it's kept in balance.

However, the apostle Paul outlined the only enduring motivation for obedience: "Christ's love compels us" (2 Corinthians 5:14). Rather than a duty-driven or formula-driven life, Christ calls us to a love-compelled life. Only that which we do out of a grateful heart will truly last; everything else is just hay and stubble. When we rest securely in God's amazing love for us, we no longer have to fabricate acts of obedience to impress or bribe Him into giving us what we want. When our hearts rest securely in God's amazing love, the noise of this world grows strangely quiet, and we can *truly hear* what God is saying, how He is directing our steps. When our hearts rest securely in God's love, our mouths speak words of encouragement and our bank accounts become tools in the kingdom. All that we have, all that we are, is available to the One to whom we owe it all.

As Jesus said, "If you love me, you will obey what I command" (John 14:15). I don't think He said that in an angry tone. I don't think He meant, "If you really love Me, *prove it* by obeying Me." I think Jesus was saying, "If you love Me, you'll spend time with Me, and obedience will be the natural outflow." Obedience compelled by love for God leads to a life that counts. However, obedience for one person may look completely different from another person's obedience, because Christ's love compels different people to reach out in completely different ways. Let me show you what I mean.

Like most aspiring pastors and ministry leaders, Jared and Kimberlee Dunn were excited to learn all they could in Bible college so they could return to their community and share the biblical knowledge and spiritual insight they had gained. God had something different in mind. Rather than a preaching ministry, God called them to join in

To hear "The Three Motivations for Obedience," visit www .donnapartow.com and click Audios. You can also find information about Adopt-A-Block, Free Wheelchair Missions, and other organizations motivated by the love of Christ by visiting www.donnapartow.com/charities.

weekly outreaches to the roughest neighborhoods of Sydney, Australia. Kimberlee says, "We didn't preach; we just loved and served people. We would clean houses, plant gardens, and paint over graffiti. I specifically remember cleaning out the fridge of a guy named Joe. It was probably the most disgusting thing I have ever cleaned, and yet I suddenly realized I was singing 'Here I Am to Worship.' That moment changed me forever. I realized my love for God was compelling me to serve *and* filling me with joy at the same time."

From then on, Kimberlee and her husband knew serving people in practical ways, outside the four walls of the church, would be a foundational principle for their ministry. They have modeled their program after the Adopt-A-Block outreach created by the Dream Center in Los Angeles.[2] Kimberlee explains, "Every Saturday we go out into the neighborhoods around our church. We clean, pull weeds, and do whatever we can. We are not knights in shining armor coming to rescue those less fortunate. We are just people loving and serving other people. When you love out of the overflow of God's love, with no strings attached, it changes you."

Kimberlee lights up when she talks about the Adopt-A-Block ministry. But I doubt my friend Chrissy would get very excited about it. This fashion maven and self-described *diva* bears a striking resemblance to a life-size Barbie doll. It's hard to picture her pulling her *own* weeds, let alone someone else's! She's never been on a mission trip. With two little boys underfoot, she doesn't expect to leave the country anytime soon (unless her husband wants to take her on a cruise to Mexico). But she has what I call a holy compulsion. Although she's thirty-six years old, she still frequents teen clothing shops in the mall, that is, when she's not visiting baby stores to purchase gifts for the teen mothers she's devoted her life to helping.

I can't think of anyone else who could connect so readily with troubled teen girls or care as compassionately for their babies as Chrissy does. She cheerfully fields phone calls in the middle of the night from young moms frantic over a crying baby who refuses to be comforted. Then again, the call might just be about a fight with parents or yet another conflict with the no-good boyfriend that Chrissy has spent hours trying to convince the teen to bid farewell to. Nothing these teenage girls do shocks Chrissy; she takes it all in stride, compelled by the love of God to love these girls who previously tried to find love in all the wrong ways and are paying the price. She says her love for God—and the love He's placed in her heart for these troubled teens—energizes her and compels her forward.

Lyn doesn't get excited about pulling weeds *or* chaperoning teen moms, but bring up the subject of wheelchairs, and be prepared for a passionate plea to get on board with the ministry of Free Wheelchair Mission.[3] She has a holy compulsion for wheelchairs. Lyn is determined to provide five hundred wheelchairs to handicapped people in Third World countries within the next year. Knowing Lyn as I do, I have no doubt she will fulfill her mission from God. Not because she feels duty bound to do so, not because she expects God to bless her, but because Christ's love compels her.

What is *your* holy compulsion? Not the thing you *ought to do;* not the thing you believe might really pay off or even please God so much He'll surely reward you. Not the thing you are willing to do as a sacrifice for God, but the thing you can't *not* do. For me, it's my mouth. I can't stop talking. Specifically, I can't stop talking about what God has done in my life. I have tried to stop many, many times: when I went through burnout, when I went through disillusionment, when I've returned from events that went badly (I've had my share!), when I've just been plain old tired. Time after time I've declared, "I quit! No more!"

Sometimes my husband will say to me, "Why don't you go back into banking? Ministry is just too demanding!" But we both know that will never happen because I have a holy compulsion. As long as I have breath, I know I'll be compelled to share with anyone who will listen what God has done in my life—just as Kimberlee shares with everyone the joys of pulling weeds, Chrissy gives everyone an earful about teen moms, and Lyn tries to galvanize God's people to donate wheelchairs.

So when you consider the possible ways you can let your life count, don't think simply about what you *can* do. Think about what you can't *not* do! Look to your holy compulsion, and let Christ's love compel you. I know from personal experience that nothing short of Christ's compelling love will provide the strength you'll need to press through hindrances, which will inevitably come.

Remember

It's possible to obey God for the wrong reasons. Duty-driven or formula-driven Christianity leads to burnout or disillusionment. Only love-compelled obedience will enable us to let our lives count.

Reflect

Have you ever lived the Christian life merely out of a sense of duty? Perhaps that's where you are right now. What were or are the results? Have you obeyed God because you wanted something specific from Him? Has He become your Vending Machine in Heaven? Have you ever been (or are you now) trapped in a formula-driven life? What would a love-compelled life look like for you? What is *your* holy compulsion?

Reach

Throughout the next week, consider doing everything out of love for your Lord. Forget about rewards and paybacks. Just let Him be the reason for everything you do.

Dear heavenly Father, I confess to You right now that I've not always obeyed You for the right reasons. At times I have felt dried out or burned up; now I realize I was operating simply out of duty. Going through the motions, doing things I thought I should do, just because they were the right things to do. I confess also that at times I've obeyed You just to get what I wanted. I've been guilty of trying to bargain—and even barter—with You. Forgive me, Lord. And change me. Help me to live compelled by love. Holy Spirit, help me to discover and live out my holy compulsion. I want to devote my life not to those things I can do, but to those things I just have to do, because Christ's love compels me. Amen.

12

Press Through Hindrances

Therefore, since we are surrounded by such a great cloud
of witnesses, let us throw off everything that hinders and
the sin that so easily entangles, and let us run with perseverance the race marked out for us.

HEBREWS 12:1

*I*f you think you're going to wake up tomorrow morning determined to let your life count and the universe is going to get
with the program, you are in for the infamous rude awakening. Letting your life count involves effort and perseverance, as the following
story illustrates.

While in Papua New Guinea, I met dozens of remarkable missionaries who have pressed through incredible obstacles to serve God
in foreign countries. One couple stands out in my mind: YongLam
and SheauJiuang Liaw. This couple from Malaysia felt called to the
work of Bible translation. After completing fourteen months of lin-
guistic training, they were assigned to Papua New Guinea—a nation
about the size of Arizona and Oklahoma combined, yet featuring
more than eight hundred languages. The couple was told to bring

along some medication to prevent malaria, which is rampant in Papua New Guinea.

SheauJiuang tried one type of medication, then another and another, but each one made her sick. Twice her reaction was so strong that it nearly cost her life. The missionary doctors there recommended they leave Papua New Guinea or find another location at a high-enough altitude that mosquitoes would not be an issue. Rather than quit, the couple asked their director to send them to a place in Papua New Guinea in which malaria wasn't a clear and present danger. It wasn't an easy task, but he identified a tribe on the side of a steep mountain, deep within the interior.

To access the remote village, the couple must journey first by small four-wheel-drive truck for four hours to the end of the road, and then hike one and a half hours to the first village to stay overnight. The next day they must hike another six and a half hours uphill to get to the village that has become their home.

On one trip to the village, because the road is so treacherous, they asked a gentleman who was experienced with the rutted and slippery jungle road to drive. On one hill they needed to shift into four-wheel

To learn more about pressing through hindrances, listen online to "Don't Give Up." Visit www.donnapartow.com and click Audios. You can also learn more about the Liaws and the work of Bible translation by visiting www.donnapartow .com/missions.

drive, but the driver couldn't make the change fast enough and lost control of the truck. With thirteen people on board, the truck began rolling backward faster and faster. The truck rolled over, then came to rest completely upside down. Miraculously, no one was seriously injured.

The Liaws have made this arduous trek to their village many times, and as long as God's people continue to provide the means, missionaries like the Liaws will continue to find ways to press through hindrances.

How many people do you know who would have persevered in the face of so many setbacks and hindrances? Until I became associated with Wycliffe Bible Translators, I knew very few. Now I know dozens of people who've pressed through similar obstacles to bring God's Word to the world. Of course, the Liaws' circumstances were a bit unusual. Do ordinary people like you and me need the strength to press through? Of course we do!

With a brand-new church staff position and the ink on her degree in social work still drying, Sara O'Donnell decided to organize an outreach to an inner-city soup kitchen. She promised to bring six volunteers. Unfortunately, just days before the outreach, no one had signed up to help. "In a church of five thousand, I hadn't successfully recruited one person." Not exactly an illustrious beginning! Yet Sara knew what God had called her to do, and she knew that her mission was to help church members make outreach a lifestyle. Determined to follow through on her commitment and undeterred by the disappointing response, Sara convinced one reluctant woman to go along with her.

That woman, too, caught the vision and got on fire for outreach.

That's when God put Sara to the test. He laid it on her heart to organize a massive outreach requiring more than one thousand volunteers. She laughs as she recalls, "I had tried to organize one outreach for six people and couldn't even come up with it, and now God was directing me to commit to eighty different outreach opportunities [to be conducted over the course of one month] requiring one thousand people. I thought, *I must be totally insane.* People were saying, 'I don't think we can do this!' It was a leap of faith for me. This project was ten times larger than anything we could realistically do, which is why I *knew* it was God."

Over the course of one month, Sara recruited 1,036 volunteers who served more than 3,000 hours in the community and donated 7,602 diapers, 454 sticks of deodorant, and 2,403 pounds of pasta, beans, and canned fruit. But none of that would have happened if Sara had not pressed through the initial roadblocks, not the least of which was the discouraging response to her first project.

God has set before each of us a unique race to run. It may not be in the jungles of Papua New Guinea or in inner-city rescue missions, but, nevertheless, we'll have to run it with perseverance if we expect to finish. We'll also have to throw off everything that hinders us. According to Webster's dictionary, *to hinder* means "to interrupt; to prevent from moving forward or to slow down." If the Enemy of your soul can't stop you from running the race God has set before you, he'll settle for slowing you down to keep you from letting your life count. Too many of us lose it right here. The slightest little hindrance, and we conclude, "Oh, well, it must not be God's will. He's must be closing the door." So be alert to a deluge of interruptions, distractions, obstacles—the things that slow you down and prevent you from moving forward—and persevere.

How can we determine if the obstacle comes from God, who is closing the door, or it if it is from the Enemy, who wants to keep us from letting our lives count? I once asked that very question of Kevin Reeves, an evangelist who travels around the world, often to nations that are considered closed to the gospel. He said it's simple. "The *first word* holds the key, so I listen intently for God's voice. I must be absolutely certain of what He's telling me to do. Then, once I've locked on to the mission, no matter what else happens, I don't let go. I never give up, never give up, never, never give up. If I encounter a closed door, I *kick that door down!*"

God's Word never promises that the universe will make it easy for us to follow Jesus. In fact, it tells us to persevere: "Throw off everything that hinders" (Hebrews 12:1). It doesn't say, "Don't worry! I'm going to set up your life so that you can never be hindered because you're just so precious. I don't want you inconvenienced, so I'm going to exempt you from the devices of the Enemy who wants to rob you of the joy of letting your life count." Not even close. God's Word makes it plain that finishing the race requires a conscious decision to actively *throw off*—not casually brush aside or quickly flick away—whatever gets in our way.

When we are running the race God intends—not off doing our own thing for God but simply being obedient to what He has told us to do—God will take the hindrances that come our way and use them for His glory. If we let Him.

In fact, the more hindrances, the greater the impossibility. The greater the impossibility, the greater the possibility for God to perform a miracle. So don't resent hindrances. Don't be surprised when they come. Be determined to throw them off. When people say, "It's impossible" or "I can't do it," what they're really saying is "There are too many hindrances." Actually, that's great, because when we overcome an "impossible" obstacle, the world sees God working through us to accomplish the impossible. I once heard Jim Cymbala from the Brooklyn Tabernacle say, "If you can explain it, God's not in it."

If you're reading these pages because you sense God is nudging you to let your life count, expect to face some hindrances. You may have grand intentions of reading a chapter a day in this book, then implementing one of the suggestions at the end of each chapter. But then:

- The kids get sick on the day you were going to take an estranged friend to lunch to resolve the difficulty in your relationship.
- Plans for a baby-sitter fall through almost every time you're supposed to volunteer at the battered women's shelter.
- The casserole you baked for a shut-in burned in the oven.

Decide right now that nothing is going to hinder you from finishing what you've started. If God convicts you about tithing or exercising or getting involved in some form of outreach, don't give up. Instead, *write down* what you feel God is calling you to do. I've found this really helps me stay on track. If I'm listening to a sermon or praying or whatever and I sense God prompting me to do something, I write it down. Once I've done so, I've taken a tangible step of commitment, which makes it more difficult for me to give up. We've got to toughen up!

God has told us up-front that hindrances will come. We're going to be hindered, and if we're *not* being hindered, guess what? There's only one explanation—there's nothing to hinder. We're not doing anything! There's not a Christian anywhere whose life counts who hasn't faced the same obstacles and hindrances—and many have faced far more than we can imagine. Press through and grow stronger! When you're ready for serious growth, get ready to dare to do the thing you dread.

Remember

If you want to let your life count, you will have to press through hindrances. Fortunately, God can help you overcome those hindrances, bringing greater glory to Himself. Don't be surprised when they come. Be determined to throw them off.

Reflect

What are some obstacles you have faced as you've tried to run the race of life? Can you think of a time when you gave up and then realized you should have pressed through? What were the results? Can you think of a time when you pressed through despite tremendous difficulties? What was the result? If you're not being hindered, is it possible that you are not in the race at all?

Reach

Think of something you gave up doing because you faced too many hindrances. Pray and consider whether or not you need to get back in that race.

Dear heavenly Father, empower me, by Your Holy Spirit, to throw off everything that hinders and the sin that so easily entangles so that I will run with perseverance the race marked out for me. Help me to fix my eyes on Jesus, the author and perfecter of my faith. Forgive me for those times when I've failed to discern whether You were closing the door or the Enemy was hindering me. Help me to be more sensitive to the Holy Spirit's leading in the future. I know that He is my counselor and will not steer me wrong. Grant me wisdom to know if there is anything I've walked away from that I need to return to or any "impossible" situations that would be very possible to face with Your grace enabling. Amen.

13

Dare to Do the Thing You Dread

For God did not give us a spirit of timidity, but a spirit of power, of love and of self-discipline. So do not be ashamed to testify about our Lord.

2 TIMOTHY 1:7–8

My family is pureblooded Irish, and as you likely know, there has been a struggle between Catholics and Protestants in a divided Ireland for most of the last century. So the fact that I, raised as an Irish Catholic, routinely attend a not specifically Catholic, nondenominational church makes some of my relatives a little uncomfortable. So other than my initial (and rather obnoxious) evangelistic fervor, I intentionally kept quiet about my faith. Why? Because I dreaded the response I might get.

I especially dreaded talking to my parents because I didn't want to offend or upset them. But when I received the news that my father was hospitalized with congestive heart failure, I knew I couldn't live another day controlled by dread. So I picked up the phone with great reluctance and had a beautiful conversation with my father about God, heaven, and where my dad would be spending eternity. After praying with him, I went to bed feeling total peace, assured that my father will be waiting in heaven for me.

I had lived in dread for twenty-five years over a conversation that lasted less than twenty-five minutes. I had been robbed of peace and missed the opportunity to let my life count where it matters most— with my *own* family. Very often, dread has the effect of immobilizing us; dread causes us to put off doing what we should do.

Dread and the procrastination that results from it are far more destructive than most people realize. The resulting emotional and mental exhaustion drains the life out of us. Dread robs us of joy, and joy is the source of our strength (see Nehemiah 8:10). A job well done typically yields a good night's sleep, but what we leave undone keeps us tossing and turning. It's not what we do but what we leave undone that haunts our quiet moments. It's those unfinished tasks, those un-spoken words.

Have you ever put something off for months or years and, as a result, experienced torment? You had no rest, then you finally did the stupid thing, and it took you a few hours. Weren't you left wondering why you put it off for so long? Didn't you regret all that time you let dread rob you of joy, strength, and peace? Ninety-nine times out of a hundred, sooner or later we'll have to face that thing we dread. If you want to let your life count, routinely decide to do the things you dread, and to do them sooner rather than later.

What do you dread? What do you procrastinate over?

- making a phone call
- going to the doctor
- getting your house in order
- going back to school
- changing jobs
- starting your own business
- launching into a new area of ministry
- confronting a friend or relative

It's amazing how many of us dread getting out of our comfort zones or doing anything that might enable us to let our lives *count*. Yet few of us dread doing pointless stuff that *doesn't count*, such as watching television or surfing the Internet. Interesting, isn't it?

If you want your life to count, then you absolutely positively will have to do things you dread.

Some days I even dread getting out of bed in the morning. Maybe you do too. Guess why that dread comes over us? God is not the one whispering in our ears, *Hit the Snooze button; it's gonna be another miserable day. You can't face it. Go back to bed.* Who do you think whispers those lies in your head? Who's the Father of Lies? (See John 8:44.)

The Enemy of our souls fills our heads with that garbage, because he dreads the prospect that we might jump out of bed in the morning ready to tackle the day and let our lives count. Instead, there we are. Snooze, snooze, snooze. *That* was the half hour we were going to spend in prayer, gone forever because we just kept snoozing.

Believe it or not, one of my nicknames used to be the Dead Woman Walking. That's what I was. I was dead because my entire life was filled with dread. Then I finally figured out that the devil was pawning off *his* dread on me. He dreaded the thought that the Dead Woman Walking might just come back to life. He thought he could keep me trapped in that living death forever; but I'm fond of saying, "Guess what, Devil? You got it wrong!" Because I refuse to live like that anymore.

My new motto is this: the devil should have killed me when he had the chance. I want to live the rest of my life in such a way that when my alarm goes off in the morning, the Enemy jumps to his feet and yells, "Oh no. She's up!"

When it's time to get up and face the day, it's time to get up and face the day. When your feet hit the floor tomorrow morning, be ready to do some damage. Stop telling yourself, *Someday I'm going to let my life count. Someday.* Meanwhile, you're camped out in your living room, watching television and eating potato chips. Why someday? Why not this day? Why not make a decision, right now, to deal with something you've been putting off for a long time?

You can be sure of this: dread, as a form of fear, cannot possibly be from God (see 2 Timothy 1:7). (Now, obviously, if you dread getting drunk, that's a different matter. I'm talking about dreading something you *know* you should do, even though it's difficult.) Look at the thing you dread most, because it may be the key to living a life that counts. This was certainly true for my sister. She dreaded going back to college later in life, but now she is a nurse, working in the cancer ward of a children's hospital. If she had continued living in dread, she would have been robbed of the daily opportunities to let her life count in the lives of her patients and their families.

Is the world being robbed because *you* are living controlled by dread? What do you dread? It is more than likely *the very thing that will let your life count*!

Jesus dreaded the cross. He was so overcome with dread that He sweat drops of blood, but He dared to die on the cross anyway. How can we look upon Him and say, "No, Jesus, it's too hard. I can't face sharing my faith with that person; I can't invite her to church, she might get offended. It's too hard for me to let my children go on a mission trip; they might get hurt; they will miss basketball camp. It's too hard for me to face that person I've hurt and ask for his forgiveness; he might not accept my apology." If Jesus dared to go the cross, how can we say no to anything He might ask us to do?

The choice is yours: Will you live your life consumed by dread? Or will you dare to let your life count? You may be afraid, but as you will soon discover, it's entirely possible to do it afraid.

For more encouragement to "Dare to Do the Thing You Dread," visit www.donnapartow.com and click Audios. If you need prayer support and encouragement, please reach out to the Let Your Life Count Community at www.donnapartow .com/lylc_community.

Remember

Dread, which is a form of fear, is not from God. Dread causes us to procrastinate and avoid doing those things we should be doing in order to let our lives count. So dare to do the thing you dread.

Reflect

What do you dread? Is there a conversation you've been putting off? Is there a change in your daily routine you've been avoiding or a decision you've refused to make? Is it possible that what you dread is what you most need to do?

Reach

Make a list of things you've dreaded, especially unspoken words and unfinished tasks. Resolve that *today* you will speak those words or tackle one task. What do you really have to lose by doing so? You may have more to gain than you realize.

Dear heavenly Father, I confess to You that I've allowed dread to control areas of my life. I've procrastinated and avoided doing things I know I should do in order to let my life count. Holy Spirit, I invite You to bring to my mind a conversation I've been putting off and empower me to face it. Show me changes I need to make in my daily routine so that I can move closer to the person You want me to be, whether in spirit, soul, or body, or even in the practical realm. Gentle Counselor, reveal to my heart the truth behind my dread. Is it possible that the thing I've put off because of dread is the very thing I most need to do in order to let my life count? What fears are driving me to avoid doing what needs to be done? Show me those unspoken words and those unfinished tasks that need to be resolved, and give me the grace to face them without fear. Amen.

14

Do It Afraid

To keep me from becoming conceited because of these surpassingly great revelations, there was given me a thorn in my flesh, a messenger of Satan, to torment me. Three times I pleaded with the Lord to take it away from me. But he said to me, "My grace is sufficient for you, for my power is made perfect in weakness." Therefore I will boast all the more gladly about my weaknesses, so that Christ's power may rest on me.

2 CORINTHIANS 12:7–9

My husband is nearly six foot four and wide enough to be an NFL linebacker. Yet the man is terrified of cats! A coworker once asked him to housesit, and being a great guy, Jeff agreed to help out. Then they mentioned that they have three cats. Uh-oh. They assured him the cats liked to hide and that he'd probably never see them anyway. Well, he wasn't too excited, but he knew they were counting on him. He recognized that their need was more important than his fear. He was willing to "do it afraid," as one famous preacher likes to put it.

Jeff woke up the first morning in their house and hopped in the shower. When he turned the water off, he realized all three cats were standing on the other side of the glass shower door, like a virtual axis of evil. Then he noticed there were no towels in the bathroom, but he was afraid to step out of the shower stall. So this six-foot-four man stood there naked, shivering, and immobilized by the sight of three cats. You can say all day long, "Well, that's silly. He shouldn't be afraid of cats; I'm not afraid of cats." The man is still afraid of cats. But that's not the point of this story! The point is that he served *in spite of his fear.*

Every one of us could list dozens of reasons why we're legitimately afraid to get out of the pew and see what God will do with our lives. Perhaps you're a shy person by temperament, and you tend to be afraid of new people and situations. Perhaps you have a history of botching things, so you're afraid you might end up doing more harm than good. You fear you're inadequate for the job. Many American Christians have been raised in comfortable suburban settings and are genuinely afraid of the inner city where the needs are greatest, because they watch the nightly news and it's pretty frightening. (Not to mention all the scary stuff that might happen to you in a foreign country! Yikes!) Few people *like* feeling out of place, which is inevitable whenever you reach out cross-culturally, whether that means crossing to the other side of the tracks or crossing an ocean. So let's be honest: letting your life count *will require* doing things you are afraid to do. But you can move forward anyway when you realize it's possible to serve in spite of your fear.

When Christine, a church secretary, received an e-mail requesting volunteers as part of a one-day outreach to an inner-city rescue mission, her immediate response was, "Count me out." She recalls,

> Everything about it scared me! First of all, it was in the worst neighborhood in Camden, New Jersey, which has the dubious honor of being America's most dangerous city. I've lived in southern New Jersey all my life but had never once stepped foot in that town. I wouldn't even visit the multimillion-dollar aquarium they put in along the riverbank. It's supposed to be beautiful, but I was scared to death to go. I guess I was even more afraid of the homeless people—you hear stories about how many of them have mental illnesses. I thought, *What if one of them suddenly attacks me? They don't shower. What if I can't handle it, the way they look and the way they smell? What if I just lose it? just completely fall apart?* I had no intention of going to a creepy rescue mission in America's most dangerous city. No thanks!

Well, that was two years ago. Now you can't keep Christine away from that rescue mission. Not only does she visit at least twice a month, but she actively recruits teams from her church to join her as well.

One director of urban ministries who didn't want her name used says Christine's fears are quite typical. "Before they go for the first time, everyone has basically the same fears. Poverty scares them. Dirty people scare them. Some are afraid they'll get shot or mugged. Others are afraid they'll get taken advantage of. They're scared someone is going to ask them a question about God or the Bible and they won't be able to answer it. Fear of the unknown. Fear of chipping a nail. The list of fears is never ending." She says she's honest with volunteers. "You know what? You might get hurt. You might say something stupid. You'll definitely feel totally out of your comfort zone. So what? You'll live *and* you'll have made a difference in someone else's life. That's what matters."

She claims that, in every single instance, fears are quickly alleviated. "Every group I've ever taken into the city has had a great response. I've never once taken someone and *not* had it ignite her faith. I definitely tell people to *do it afraid*."

Can I make a small confession about my fears? I'm afraid every time I walk into a room full of people and head toward the microphone. I'm afraid the audience won't like me or won't agree with everything I say, and sometimes they don't. I recently spoke at a small gathering, and afterward about a dozen people came up to me. With only one exception, every person came to offer a critique of some form or another. Yes, it hurt. Yes, it left me feeling even more insecure as I prepared for my next event, but that didn't release me from doing

Find courage by clicking Audios at www.donnapartow.com and listening free to "Do It Afraid." If you need prayer support and encouragement, please reach out to the Let Your Life Count Community at www.donnapartow.com/lylc _community.

what God has called me to do. My fears and personal insecurities are not a license to disobey God.

Too many of us spend an inordinate amount of time focusing on ourselves, even if only to pick ourselves apart. As a result, we never put ourselves in places where God can use us. If we spent half as much time serving others as we do obsessing over our insecurities, the cause of Christ would be much further along. I have met thousands of amazing Christian women all over the United States—women who have much to offer but who are not offering it to God or the world because they are literally in bondage to their fears and personal insecurities. I can't help wondering, *What would happen if, all of a sudden, we rose up out of the pews and went out into the world? What if we simply chose to do it afraid?* Can we even imagine the impact if every woman who sits in a pew on Sunday morning went out into the world on Monday morning determined to let her life count? It would be a revolution!

May I ask you something? Are you using your fears and personal insecurities as a license to disobey God? If you're not sure, let me ask a few more questions that might clarify your answer. When's the last time you felt led to do something as simple and painless as inviting someone to church, but were too afraid to act on the impulse? Why not invite someone this week?

Let's make this more challenging: when's the last time you had an opportunity to share the gospel with someone but backed away? Have you felt a tug on your heart toward short-term mission trips but talked yourself out of going? When's the last time you walked into a rough neighborhood just to hang out and chat with people? When's the last time you reached out or did anything that took you out of your comfort zone?

Gotcha! You're afraid of something.

Since I haven't met you, I won't try to guess what that fear might be. But I will tell you that I've yet to meet a person who isn't afraid of rejection, at least to some degree. Now, of course, we shouldn't be afraid of something so intangible. My husband's fear of cats—which can scratch, bite, and make you sneeze—is actually more reasonable than refusing to sing a song for fear someone might not like your voice, your style, your outfit, or even your life history. King David wrote, "The LORD is the stronghold of my life—of whom shall I be afraid?" (Psalm 27:1). God assures us, "I have chosen you and have not rejected you" (Isaiah 41:9).

If you want to let your life count, please don't use your fears and insecurities as a license to disobey God. Courage is not the absence of fear but the judgment that something else is more important than fear. The difference between Christians and the rest of the world is not that we don't have our share of issues but that we are convinced that God is greater and that it's worth risking everything to obey Him. There's no other way to let your life count. In fact, when you move forward in faith, even your problems can count.

Everyone has fears and personal insecurities. Don't use your personal insecurities as a license to disobey God. Instead, make the decision to do it afraid.

Reflect

What are some of your major fears and personal insecurities? In what way have you used them as a license to disobey God? How can you take some positive steps in the direction of doing it afraid?

Reach

Think of one thing God may be leading you to do (initiate a conversation with a stranger, speak in front of a group, and so on), and pray for God to open the door for you to do it afraid.

Dear heavenly Father, You know I'm afraid, and You know everything I'm afraid of. Yet I know You haven't given me a spirit of fear, but of love, power, and a sound mind. So obviously my fears come from within me and are played upon—and preyed upon—by the Enemy of my soul. Lord, forgive me for living controlled by fear and using my personal insecurities as a license to disobey You. Holy Spirit, show me how my fears and insecurities are hindering me from living a life that counts. Then empower me to do it afraid. Amen.

solicited so aggressively. Carla knew that no one touched that computer but her husband. Suddenly she understood why he "worked" on the computer for hours every night with the door locked. How could she have been so blind? Carla quickly hung up. She threw up and cried for hours.

When she calmed down, she clicked on the Internet History button only to discover a list of the vilest Web sites imaginable. She quickly packed bags for herself and her two little boys, then booked a flight home to stay with her parents until she could sort things out. No matter how hard she tried, she couldn't erase the horror of what she'd seen or forgive the betrayal she felt. But Carla had gotten her husband's attention by removing herself from the situation. When confronted, he confessed and began going to intensive counseling. He said he would do anything to win her back.

After living in her childhood bedroom for three months, Carla returned to her husband, who claimed to be a changed man. She was certainly a changed woman. Crushed in spirit, humiliated by the constant need to explain to the neighbors where she'd gone, and unwilling to share the truth about why, she turned into a shell of her former self. She could no longer sleep at night; she rebuffed any of her husband's attempts at intimacy—it was unthinkable to her. Her brief exposure to her husband's sin had deeply defiled her, and now she overflowed with bitterness. His problem had become her problem.

Eventually, Carla sought counseling, where she came to grips with the reality that her sinful response was ultimately more defiling to her than the sins her husband had committed against her. Today, Carla and Larry are letting their lives count—yes, even the ugliest

15

Even Your Problems Can Count

Dear friends, do not be surprised at the painful trial you
are suffering, as though something strange were happening to you. But rejoice that you participate in the sufferings of Christ, so that you may be overjoyed when his
glory is revealed.

1 PETER 4:12–13

*O*ne of the surest ways to discover the work God has uniquely
prepared for you to do is to explore the problems you've faced.
Just ask Carla. Nothing could have prepared her for what was about
to pop up on her husband's computer screen. All she wanted to do
was answer their accountant's question about last year's taxes, but
when she tried to access the information online, a deluge of pornographic images assaulted her. No matter which button she hit, more
images popped up. She screamed in panic and disgust, so the accountant asked what was happening. He hinted that someone had used that
computer to visit pornographic sites, and that's why it was now being

garbage imaginable can be redeemed by our awesome God. They serve as facilitators in a small-group study designed for those struggling with sexual addictions and for their loved ones.

If a problem-free existence were the prerequisite for living a life that counts, the entire human race would be disqualified. The problem is not that we have problems, because everybody does. The problem is what we do with the problems we've got! God never said Christians would float to heaven on the legendary and highly coveted flowery beds of ease. In fact, Jesus said, "In this world you *will* have trouble" (John 16:33, emphasis added). (Funny how no one puts *that* verse on a plaque!) Having problems doesn't disqualify us from letting our lives count. Problems, if handled properly, will make us more compassionate and more able to let our lives count. But if handled improperly, problems can render us ineffective and unproductive in our knowledge of God. What's the difference? Perspective!

Think about it. We can look at our problems from our own selfish points of view (we're all good at that!). Or we can step back and be more objective, maybe even walk a mile in another person's shoes. But if we want to let our lives count, what we ultimately need to do is "see things from [Christ's] perspective" (Colossians 3:2, MSG).

The further we get from our problems, the more realistic our perspective becomes. For example, imagine two children fighting over a section of the sandbox. To them, it's a life-and-death struggle; nothing seems more important to either of them than winning that turf war. But an astronaut flying in a space shuttle would have a completely different view of the importance of that sandbox and how it compares to the rest of the world. When we view the struggle in the sandbox from the astronaut's perspective, we quickly realize that it's not critical at all. And if we step back even further and consider it from God's vantage point, we'll see the sandbox for what it really is: less than a speck on a planet that is just one speck in one vast universe in the midst of all He has created.

Most of us can recall a situation we thought was a harrowing ordeal, only to have laughed about it years later. Vacations and parenthood are the perfect examples. When everything starts going haywire, we think the world is coming to an end. We think we'll be stuck forever in a rundown hotel room, chasing toddlers while it rains at the beach. (Even though it was completely sunny the weeks before *and* after our vacation.) Decades later, we take out the family photo album and suddenly wax nostalgic for the good ol' days. What changed? Our perspective on the problem.

What if we lived our lives with the big picture in view? What if we lived every day realizing our "momentary, light affliction" (2 Corinthians 4:17, NASB) is nothing when viewed from an eternal perspective? The more we see of God, the more we fix our eyes on eternity, on what actually matters, the easier it becomes to take daily stuff in

To read a free excerpt, "Putting Your Problems into Perspective," visit www.donnapartow.com/mmp. You can also listen to "Shining Through the Broken Places," about God's power to transform your problems into your greatest ministry opportunities. Visit www.donnapartow.com and click Audios.

stride. Most of what we get so worked up about—and I'm the worst offender—doesn't even matter. Getting stuck in traffic, showing up late for appointments, finding dirty socks on the floor, misplacing our car keys, getting our feelings hurt—these are the daily problems we obsess over. I'm embarrassed to think how much time and energy I've depleted on such trivial nonsense. How often we tear people down or beat ourselves up! When your children move out of the house, will you honestly care that they drew on the walls with crayons, didn't earn straight As, or stuffed peas under their plates?

Earlier this week, I attended the funeral for a sixty-eight-year-old man from my church. I am certain that as his wife grieved for her husband of forty-eight years, she didn't care one drop whether he had picked up after himself. Or if he played the television too loudly or watched too much football. He had suffered from Alzheimer's for several years, and his wife says that during that time she was sustained by two things: compassion and hope.

She had to imagine what it must feel like to *not remember;* she had to try to see the world from his point of view. It wasn't easy, but her perspective helped her care for her husband with great tenderness. What truly kept her going, though, was her hope of heaven. The hope that someday, every tear will be washed away, every mystery made plain, every problem resolved. But certainly not on this side of heaven.

I recently spent time crying and praying with a pastor's wife who is caring for her mother and her mother's twin sister, both of whom have Alzheimer's. This woman's denomination strongly believes that God still heals people today; her husband has taught that from the pulpit for years. However, she recently said to me, "I guess we'll just have to wait for the ultimate healing." She was referring, of course, to that moment when her mom and her aunt leave behind earth and all its problems.

Ironically, truly heart-wrenching problems have a way of putting all of life's little problems into perspective. I've yet to encounter anyone in the advanced stages of cancer, wasting away in a hospital bed, complaining that her husband never did fulfill his promise to paint the family room. Or that she had never been able to lose those last ten pounds.

So don't bemoan your "fate," and assume that your life can't count because of the problems you face. You are *not* the only person to end up divorced or with wayward children. You're not the only person with grown kids who've walked away from God and won't even speak to you. You're not the only person who's ever been fired unfairly from a job or suffered financial setbacks. You're not the only person whose church has hurt her feelings or whose doctor gave her a painful diagnosis.

So rather than sitting around feeling sorry for yourself, wondering how on earth something like that could happen to *you*, why not look around and prayerfully ask, *Who else is facing this or a similar problem? How can I help them? How can we encourage one another?* Hey, as long as you're in the same boat, you might just as well start rowing together! Besides, with God's grace, you can *always* rise above your circumstances. As I said earlier, hard times and heartaches can't keep God from using you to make a difference in this world; in fact, they may be the very things that God will use to let your life count, but it may mean that you'll have to be willing to sacrifice.

Everyone has problems, not just you! Far from disqualifying you for kingdom service, your problems, if handled correctly, will be the very things that will enable you to let your life count.

Do you tend to overreact to your problems, blowing things out of proportion? Do you tell yourself no one else has it as tough as you? How can you get a more realistic perspective on your problems? What problems, large or small, are you facing right now?

Make a list of problems in your life. Now identify other people who are going through similar trials. Reach out to help them, or find a way to help one another. (You might also want to check out my previous book, *Soon to Be a Major Motion Picture*, which is all about putting your problems into perspective.)

Dear heavenly Father, I'm not thankful for the problems I've faced or even the problems I'm facing right now. But I'm profoundly grateful that, because I know You, it's possible that even my problems can count. Thank You, Lord, for being a Redeemer, for working all things together for good in my life. Yes, even the hard things I'd prefer not to live through. I confess my tendency to feel sorry for myself. I confess that sometimes I lose perspective and feel like I'm the only person in the world who has problems. Forgive me for not retaining an eternal perspective. Holy Spirit, open my eyes to people around me who are facing similar or even worse problems. Bring creative ideas to my mind concerning how I can let my life count by helping others. Amen.

16

Be Willing to Sacrifice

Therefore, I urge you, brothers, in view of God's mercy,
to offer your bodies as living sacrifices, holy and pleasing
to God—this is your spiritual act of worship.

ROMANS 12:1

*I*n order to let our lives life count, we must be willing to make sacrifices. There really isn't an easier way.

When God asked Abraham to sacrifice his son Isaac, Abraham didn't miss a step. In simple obedience, he informed his son that they were going up the mountain to make a sacrifice to God. The two climbed the mountain, and Isaac observed, "The fire and wood are here...but where is the lamb for the burnt offering?" (Genesis 22:7). Abraham told him that God would provide the lamb (verse 8). Even though Abraham didn't understand how, by faith he believed that God had an answer to this impossible situation. To me the most significant aspect of this story is not what Abraham did, but what he didn't do.

But first, let's look at what he did: In verses 9 and 10 we see that Abraham built the altar, tied up his son, placed him on the altar, then raised the knife to make the sacrifice. At the last second, God said, "Do not lay a hand on the boy.... Do not do anything to him. Now I know that you fear God, because you have not withheld from me your son, your only son" (verse 12). In other words, God told him, "This was a test. This was only a test. I've got the solution: the ram is in the bushes" (see verse 13). Whew! That was close.

That's what Abraham did and how God responded. What didn't he do? He didn't *look for the ram in the bushes.* He wasn't looking for the easy way out. Maybe some of us walk away from this story with the wrong message. We figure that since God put the ram in the bushes for Abraham, He'll do that for us too. I'm guilty of this myself. Pretty much *any* time God asks me to sacrifice, to do anything difficult, to let go of anything I'd rather keep or anyone I'd rather hold on to, I look around in the bushes to see if He's provided the ram, hoping it's just a test, hoping that God doesn't really want me to make any kind of sacrifice.

I've found that God often calls us to sacrifice our bright ideas about how He should run our lives. Apparently Abraham had already learned that lesson the hard way. Many years earlier, God had promised to give Abraham a son. But God didn't move fast enough, so Abraham (then called Abram) and his wife, Sarah (then called Sarai), decided maybe there was an easier way to obtain what God had promised. They devised their own plan, in which Abram slept with Sarai's maidservant, in hopes that the servant would get pregnant and Abram would have a child (Genesis 16:1–2). If you're unfamiliar with the outcome of that story, it turns out pretty much as you might predict: Sarah ends up resenting the maidservant and her son and insists that Abraham get rid of them (Genesis 21:9–13).

While it must have felt like a huge sacrifice for Abraham and Sarah to wait until their old age to have the promised son, waiting upon God's timing would have been far easier than coping with the mess they created by looking for an easier way. The human race is still dealing with the aftermath of their bright idea, because Abraham's two sons—the one Abram got "the easy way" (Ishmael) and the one he had to wait for (Isaac)—became two races, the Jews and the Arabs, who to this day are at each other's throats. Ironically, the "easier way" often ends up causing far more hardship and heartache than the way that will require us to sacrifice something.

Maybe God is asking you to make a sacrifice, to let go of your timetable, your agenda, or something else you don't want to let go of. Maybe it's a relationship you need to walk away from or a relationship you need to restore by sacrificing your pride. Maybe it's a habit, an addiction, or just an annoying personality trait. Maybe there's a flaw in your character that you need to kill, that you need to lay down on the altar and let die. Maybe you need to sacrifice junk food or love of food in general. Or television. Surfing the Internet. Many of us need to sacrifice our love of money and hunger for success. We need to sacrifice our never-ending need to have life go *our* way *right now,* our demand to be heard, our demand to be right or to be understood. Some of us need to let go of the desire to control our time, our money, our agendas—even our kids' lives.

Sometimes God provides us with a ram in the bushes, and we're off the hook. However, when God does so, it's called a *miracle* because more often than not, He requires us to go through with the sacrifice. So stop looking for an easier way to become who God wants you to be or to do what God has called you to do. If you want to let your life count, stop looking for a ram in the bushes.

I don't know what sacrifices God is calling you to make in your own life, but a life that counts requires sacrifice. The apostle Paul urged us to sacrifice: "Therefore, I *urge* you, brothers, in view of God's mercy, to offer your bodies as *living sacrifices,* holy and pleasing to God—this is your spiritual act of worship" (Romans 12:1, emphasis added). Peter noted that we are to be a holy priesthood "offering spiritual sacrifices acceptable to God through Jesus Christ" (1 Peter 2:5). Ugandan pastor Jackson Senyonga points out, "Perhaps the reason there is so little fire in the faith of American Christians is because the fire of God only falls on sacrifice."[1] His country is enjoying a massive nationwide revival, but it came only after Christians in Uganda sacrificed their personal interests to devote hours to prayer, fasting, and evangelism. *Sacrifice* is a dirty word in the United States, even in our churches. We are so fixated on grace, so delighted with our comfortable Christianity, that we think it's beneath us to sacrifice through fasting, praying for extended periods, giving until it hurts, living in simplicity, choosing to forgive our enemies, or putting others first. However, these are the spiritual sacrifices the Bible urges all believers to make.

I recently offered a small sacrifice to God by saying yes to a missions' exploration trip to Turkey when I would have much preferred to stay home. Missiologists list Turkey as one of the least evangelized nations on the planet.[2] While there, I visited a city with a population of one and a half million people that has only one missionary couple working there. One. As I listened to the husband, Bob, share their story,

I marveled at the sacrifices they make—far from home, separated from any other believers, slandered in the national media, blacklisted in the local community, hounded by police and Islamic extremists. That's the easy part! The hard part is continuing to walk by faith when they see no visible fruit from their labors. After years of missionary service, they know of one believer in the city. One.

As he spoke to our group, Bob quoted from a book by Dr. William Miller, who had served as a missionary in neighboring Iran for forty-three years. Dr. Miller observed, "Sometimes you're just picking up stones." That's what Bob felt he was doing: just picking up stones. In other words, he hadn't even been able to plant seeds yet. He and his wife were still clearing the field to make it suitable for planting, watering, and so on.

My heart leaped for joy at the mention of Dr. Miller, who was, and is, so dear to me. Bob was initially skeptical when I professed to have known Dr. Miller personally, since he had lived in another century. True enough. He was born in 1892 in rural Kentucky. Nevertheless, I met him in 1982 when he was living in a Philadelphia retirement home.

Dr. Miller had walked thousands of miles, journeying from village

To hear "The Call to Sacrifice," a complete message on the life of Abraham, visit www.donnapartow.com and click Audios. You can also take our survey, "Self-Indulgent or Sacrificial?" at www.donnapartow.com/sacrifice.

to village, separated from his family for months at a time, just picking up stones, trying to remove Muslim misconceptions about the Christian faith. It wasn't until after his retirement that he finally saw an initial harvest among Iranians. When he was in his eighties and nineties, he began to receive letters and visits from Iranians who had come to know Christ through Dr. Miller's years of sacrificial ministry. He was living proof that God's Word is true: "Let us not become weary in doing good, for at the proper time we will reap a harvest if we do not give up" (Galatians 6:9).

Dr. Miller sacrificed his life, even as others are doing today, not knowing if he would ever see the fulfillment of God's promises concerning the Muslim people he ministered among. Bob confided, with tears in his eyes, how weary he had become lately, and how my information about the outcome of Dr. Miller's life was exactly the encouragement he needed to press on. Until that beautiful God-ordained moment, I honestly had no idea what on earth I was doing in Turkey. I had gone simply because I felt God had prompted me to go. But God had sent me halfway around the world just to encourage that one missionary. It was worth whatever small sacrifices I had to make in time, money, and discomfort to let my life count in that spiritually barren land.

While in Turkey I also visited the underground cities and cave churches of Cappadocia, where Christians hid during the second-century Roman persecution that killed eight million people. I visited the ruins of giant stadiums where Christians were thrown to wild animals as a form of entertainment. We met one Turkish believer who had become a Christian at the age of fifteen. He was arrested the following year at the urging of his own father and tortured with electric shocks that left him blind in one eye. When someone asked if he'd ever been beaten, he said, "Of course. Whenever they arrest you, they beat you." He said this as casually as an American Christian would if asked, "Have you ever been to a potluck supper?" Beatings are just a routine part of being a Christian in many countries.

Our contemporary Western perspective on Christianity is unique in history. In the past, saints of old considered sacrifice an essential part of their faith journeys. Spiritual pioneers such as John Wesley wouldn't even ordain a man who didn't fast twice a week. Imagine the astonishment of Christians who laid down their lives in the gladiator arenas if they were to walk into a church today only to discover a stadium-sized building full of Christians who wouldn't dream of laying aside their personal agendas long enough to attend a weekly prayer meeting, let alone laying down their lives in death.

I don't know what sacrifices God is calling you to make. Perhaps He's only asking you for the sacrifice of a broken and contrite heart. That's the ideal starting point and a place to which I've often had to return. But King David, who said God would not despise such a simple offering, also said, "I insist on paying the full price. I will not… sacrifice a burnt offering that costs me nothing" (1 Chronicles 21:24). Sometimes God just wants our hearts; other times He wants our bodies, our money, our time, and everything else! What sacrifice is God prompting *you* to make?

Maybe it's the sacrifice of laboring in obscurity, with little reward and no accolades. In that case, you'll need to remember that overshadowed doesn't mean overlooked.

Remember

As Christians, we are called to offer spiritual sacrifices, even offering ourselves as living sacrifices. There is no easy way to become the person God has called you to be, no easy way to do what God has called you to do, no other way to let your life count.

Reflect

Would you describe your life as a living sacrifice? Would people describe your lifestyle as sacrificial or self-indulgent? When is the last time you made a spiritual sacrifice to God? When was the last time you sacrificed anything (time, money, pride, agenda, food, and so on) to let your life count? What changes do you need to make in your life?

Reach

Why not ask God what form of spiritual sacrifice He might want you to offer *this week*?

Dear heavenly Father, I must admit that the idea of sacrifice doesn't appeal to me. I would much rather think that sacrifice was only for the

Old Testament. Yet Your Word commands me—yes, in the New Testament—to offer spiritual sacrifices, even to offer my entire body as a living sacrifice to You. Forgive me for looking for that ram in the bushes—that easier way than the way of sacrifice, that way of taking up my cross and following Jesus. Holy Spirit, I invite You to search not only my heart but my lifestyle as well. Show me where I've chosen self-indulgence over sacrificial living. Open my heart to the spiritual sacrifices You are calling me to offer—whether it's my time, money, pride, personal agenda, food, or whatever else You want to show me. Lord, I truly want to let my life count, and I am willing to sacrifice as part of that process. Amen.

17

Overshadowed Doesn't Mean Overlooked

Your Father, who sees what is done in secret, will reward you.

MATTHEW 6:18

The Johnsons are a musical family. When Marianne, the mother, plays piano, it's not a performance, it's an electrifying event. The father, David, strums anything with strings on it, from violin to cello. Four of their children—a drummer, a flutist, a violinist, and a trumpet player—join them on stage at Christian conferences around the country. They travel pretty much full-time in their RV, home-schooling their children on the road.

Did I mention that they have five children?

Sarah, their second oldest, has never had any interest in or talent for music. Of course, she traveled with the rest of the family, staying in the background, helping with lighting, sound, tape and CD sales, and whatever else needed to be done. Sarah worked hard. Most of all, she worked hard not to be resentful. She wanted a normal life, going to a normal school with a normal family rather than attending RV school with her extraordinarily gifted clan. It wasn't easy.

I met the Johnsons shortly after Sarah had run away from home in honor of her seventeenth birthday. Her parents never saw it coming. But Sarah had been overshadowed for too long, so she went off in search of a place to belong. Although her parents had no idea where she had gone, God followed her everywhere she went. Actually, to use Sarah's words, "He hemmed me in behind and before [Psalm 139:5]! I had memorized that psalm as a little girl, but honestly didn't know what it meant. But everywhere I ran to, I somehow stumbled upon something that pointed me to God. I was amazed how many Christians crossed my path. I could totally tell that God was looking out for me, caring for me in special ways."

Altogether Sarah was away for eight weeks, long enough for her to realize that being overshadowed by her family didn't mean she'd been overlooked by God. "I can't say I'm glad I ran away. I definitely wouldn't recommend it! But God used it in my life." It was during that time that Sarah said she realized being a musician wasn't the only way to let her life count. "I began looking inside, asking what did *I* want to do with my life. That's when I realized I wanted to be a midwife. I had been there when my mom gave birth, and it was so miraculous."

Sarah is now in her last year of nursing school, and she plans to follow that with training to become a midwife. She still attends her family's concerts from time to time. "The resentment is gone now because I've found my place. I think if I hadn't, that root of bitterness would have stayed forever, eating away at me all the time."

Sarah's story reminds me of what happened to Judah, who was

one of Joseph's older brothers. It seems everyone knows the story of wonderful Joseph and how his awful brothers sold him into slavery. No less a Hollywood powerhouse than Steven Spielberg's Dream-Works produced a movie about the ordeal entitled *Joseph: King of Dreams*. There's even a Broadway show called *Joseph and the Amazing Technicolor Dreamcoat*. No doubt about it, Joseph's dramatic, larger-than-life story captures our imagination. It also overshadowed everyone around him, including Judah, who, in many ways, is ultimately a much more significant figure in the history of our faith.

Judah is not only overlooked by Broadway and movie producers, he was also overlooked by his own father, who seemed to think that Joseph and only Joseph had an amazing future. But did being over-shadowed by Joseph and overlooked by his father mean that Judah had been overlooked by God? Far from it! God chose Judah and his brothers to become the twelve tribes of Israel. These men—yes, these same guys who sold Joseph into slavery—were the ones with whom God established a special relationship out of all the nations of the earth. (Just goes to show that making colossal mistakes doesn't dis-qualify you from letting your life count!)

Throughout the conquest of the Promised Land, all the tribes looked to the tribe of Judah for leadership and assistance. They went bravely to the front line of the battle, leading the charge (Numbers 10:14). God confirmed His confidence in Judah's family when the people inquired: " 'Who of us shall go first to fight against the Ben-jamites?' The LORD replied, 'Judah shall go first' " (Judges 20:18).

God declared that Judah's descendants will always have someone sitting on the throne. "The scepter will not depart from Judah" (Genesis 49:10). The scepter stands for the ruling power of royalty. God chose David, a son of Jesse of the tribe of Judah, to be king over His people, Israel. He did not choose a descendant of Joseph. One of the strongest statements concerning God's perspective on this family occurs in Psalm 78:67–68: "Then [God] rejected the tents of Joseph, he did not choose the tribe of [Joseph's son] Ephraim; but he chose the tribe of Judah, Mount Zion, which he loved."

Judah's descendants became the most powerful and important of all the tribes, not just throughout the Old Testament, but in the New Testament as well. "For it is clear that our Lord descended from Judah" (Hebrews 7:14). Jesus is called the Lion of the tribe of Judah (Revelation 5:5); He's not the Lion of the tribe of Joseph!

Even though Judah was overshadowed by Joseph and overlooked by his own father, God used him to make a significant difference in the world. The moral of the story is this: you don't have to be at the center of attention for your life to count. It's not always the person who makes the biggest splash or who wears the sharpest clothes or

There is an online support network for women who are committed to raising the next generation for Christ. Teaching, encouragement, and prayer support are available at www .donnapartow.com/muskox. You can also listen to two additional messages, "Overshadowed Doesn't Mean Overlooked" and "Generations," by visiting www.donnapartow.com and clicking Audios.

who receives the most accolades who counts in the long term. Judah plugged away, year after year, and not only did his *own* life count, but his influence continued to be felt for generations.

We're not told why God chose Judah's descendants over Joseph's. This is obviously conjecture, but I can't help wondering if Joseph became so enamored of ruling Egypt that he failed to invest in the lives of his own children and grandchildren. Perhaps he overshadowed his children just as he had overshadowed his brothers. Perhaps his children rebelled because their dad's "important work" overshadowed them, and so they wanted nothing to do with religion.

This is one of the greatest mistakes I've made and one that is far too common among Christians who earnestly desire to let their lives count. (Maybe it's because we're so afraid our contributions might be overshadowed by others who are "accomplishing more"?) We can become so engrossed with "important" work that we neglect our own family members who later resent that "Mommy was too busy serving Jesus to serve us dinner." Last weekend, Jeff and I had planned to have our annual family getaway at a mountain cabin in Flagstaff, Arizona. We were all looking forward to a break. Instead, Jeff (an architect) spent the entire weekend cooped up in his home office, working on free projects for various friends, and I worked on this book day and night. We hardly saw each other, and neither of us slept much. The kids were nowhere around.

I cried for hours Sunday night as I realized that, *once again,* our own family got left behind as we knocked ourselves out for everyone on the planet except one another. As we seek to let our lives count, let's be certain that we don't leave our own families behind. And yes,

I plan to make major changes! Most of all, I need to remind myself daily that what counts is *not* the stuff that gets the most immediate appreciation or applause. It's often what we do quietly—in our own homes, with no fanfare—that matters most.

My friend Judy never misses an opportunity to remind people of this truth. Her children are grown and gone now, but as she says, "They treat me like a queen because I put them first." Her life may have been overshadowed by women in the community who achieved more or by women in the church who accomplished more, but her humble service to her family and her King has not been overlooked by them or Him.

She offers this sage advice: "For mothers, the number one way to let our lives count is to raise responsible, accountable children who become independent of us and dependent on God. If we provide a home that is safe for all family members, we are letting our lives count. Using the Bible as our guide, our homes should be in order and the family should flourish within the walls. That means mothers must see this as a career, even if they work outside the home. We should take an active role in our church and community, but not to the detriment of our family. If we mess up raising our children and creating a home for them to enjoy, none of our other accomplishments will count for much."

Perhaps the reason our lives will not be judged until this earth passes away is because the full measure of our lives cannot be taken until the last person we have impacted has died. As my father nears death, this thought has become more real to me. Dad invested in my life; now I need to make it top priority to invest in my children's lives.

My father's impact will continue through my descendants *and* the descendants of every life in which my life counts, as long as that influence remains. That which was overshadowed in life will not be overlooked in eternity. As Jesus said, those things we do in secret will be brought out of the shadows into the light to be rewarded openly (see Matthew 6:4–18).

Perhaps you were overshadowed by one of your siblings or overlooked by your parents. Or maybe you were overshadowed throughout school by classmates who were smarter, faster, better looking, more popular, or more talented. Maybe you've been overshadowed and overlooked at your place of employment. Or maybe you're a stay-at-home mother and you feel that your contributions are perpetually overlooked. Stay faithful. Invest in the lives of your family members and those God brings across your path. In fact, let every season count.

Remember

Being overshadowed doesn't mean being overlooked. It's not always the person who gets the most attention whose life counts most. Those things you do for His kingdom, even if they are overshadowed now, will be rewarded openly in eternity.

Reflect

Have you ever been overshadowed? How did that make you feel? Do you ever feel overlooked by God?

How does it make you feel to know that it's not always the person who *seems* to count whose life has the greatest impact?

Reach

Be alert to someone who may feel overshadowed by people or overlooked by God. Reach out to affirm that her life counts, perhaps sharing the insights you've gained from the life of Judah.

Dear heavenly Father, I admit that at times I've struggled with feeling overshadowed. I've noted the positions and opportunities You've granted to others and wondered if You've forgotten all about me. Lord, sometimes it's so hard to labor faithfully in obscurity when I feel like my contributions are constantly overshadowed and overlooked. Help me to look to You and not to other people or earthly accolades. Father, I offer to You all those things I do in secret, all those things no one knows about. I trust that You do see and that You will reward me openly someday. Holy Spirit, open my eyes to see those around me who feel overshadowed and overlooked. Help me to be an encouragement to them. Amen.

18

Let Every Season Count

There is a time for everything,

and a season for every activity under heaven.

ECCLESIASTES 3:1

*E*very season of life presents a legitimate excuse for why we can't let our lives count, doesn't it?

Let's take a hypothetical Sunday-school class in which the teacher asks for volunteers to work a few hours each week at the church's new outreach center, which offers everything from food and clothing to after-school tutoring and computer- and job-skills training. Kristin, a twenty-something mother with three young children at home, says she can't volunteer because she's in such a demanding season of life. Ironically, the woman sitting next to her, sixty-plus Dorothy, doesn't volunteer either, because she's had her turn. Of course, she doesn't tell the teacher this, but she and the other women in her adult community talk about it all the time because they understand each other. Dorothy survived all the demanding seasons of life, and now it's time for her to relax and let the younger people do the work. Dan, the attorney, and his wife, Candy, the real estate agent, can't volunteer either. He recently opened his own practice, and so for now anyway, it's nose to the grindstone seven days a week. Candy says the housing market is booming. Since one never knows when the trend might turn, it's essential for her to make hay while the sun shines. No one even dares to suggest Mildred, the poor woman, assume any responsibilities. Her constant health challenges keep her fully occupied. She finds children unnerving, and unless those already down-and-out people want to discuss how much she suffers with migraine headaches, chronic back pain, and fibromyalgia, it's hard to imagine what she would have in common with them.

If we're not careful, our lives will pass and we'll have done nothing more than pass the time. If we want our lives to count, we'll look for opportunities rather than excuses, which is what my friend Aly has done. Although she homeschools her three children, she doesn't use that demanding responsibility as an excuse for not volunteering. Instead, she involves her children in ministry, viewing it as the ultimate teaching opportunity. Aly loves cooking and showing hospitality, so anytime my ministry needs someone to provide refreshments, Aly and her children spring into action. Aly's family also played host, on two separate occasions, to international guests of my ministry—a woman from Uganda, who stayed in their home for nearly three weeks, and a young man from Papua New Guinea, who captivated her children for a week with stories of spiders and snakes and what God was doing in the lives of people in his tribal village.

My friend Betty also chose not to give in to her season-of-life excuses. When she was seventy-nine years old, she decided to teach a weekly Bible study at her home church. Betty died recently, and at her funeral, her pastor mentioned that she had endured chronic pain from severe arthritis, a fact she had never mentioned to me in all the years that I knew her. Betty had great difficult walking but had never uttered a word of complaint and certainly had never used her physical limitations as an excuse to limit her service to the King. Betty knew how much I relied on her love and prayers, so she always attended my events in the Phoenix area, even though she required special transportation because of her limited range of motion and need for a walker. Betty had a truckload of legitimate excuses to sit home feeling sorry for herself, but she refused to do so. Instead, she remained active in the prayer ministry of her church until shortly before her death.

What better excuse could there be for a woman to stay focused on the home front than a house full of teenagers? With two teens at home, Joy was convinced she had too much on her plate, so she asked the Lord to take control of her calendar. Much to her surprise, He did not eliminate any activities; in fact, He added one. She joined a small group at her church composed of six women who seemingly had nothing in common and whose ages ranged from twenty-one to seventy-nine. Single, married, divorced, and widowed—they were a diverse lot. When the twenty-one-year-old got married, everyone attended. Then they had a surprise eightieth birthday party for their oldest member, with more than fifty people in attendance. Shortly afterward the woman's health failed, and the entire group routinely gathered around her bedside to pray with her. Even when her condition deteriorated so severely that she had to be transferred to a nursing home, the women took turns visiting to assure her she'd never be forgotten.

Joy sends a box of chocolates to the widow every year on her wedding anniversary, because that's what the woman's husband had always done. Joy's friend is also now in a nursing home, but Joy keeps in touch and plans to keep sending those chocolates until the Lord takes her friend home. Joy says, "I believe God let my life count in a major way in the lives of these six women. Not one of these ways was a big deal in and of itself, but the love and trust they built between us is immeasurable."

Seniors have had a profound impact on the life of seventeen-year-old Carissa, whose mother worked at an assisted-living facility for several years. Carissa spent many hours visiting the residents, listening as they shared their life stories and life lessons. One gentleman in particular left a permanent mark on her life: Charles Sims, or Colonel Sims as everyone called the retired army officer.

Carissa says, "I think he was typical of an eighty-year-old man who had been in the army thirty-plus years. Rough, tough, and matter-of-fact personality. The colonel was disciplined with money, true to his family, and faithful to God. Everywhere he went he made sure to leave behind a trail of tidbits for those who would take an interest and listen to the wisdom he had stored up inside over the years."

As Carissa watched the colonel interacting with his wife, Ann, and everyone else he encountered, she knew she'd discovered not only a role model, but a font of wisdom. "Whenever I had a major decision to make, I would go and sit with the colonel for a while. During my freshman year, I was contemplating taking a mission trip with our church youth group. I knew he had traveled the world and would be sure to give me sound advice." When Carissa told him what she had in mind, he poured out his heart for the world with such conviction that she felt she could never be the same again.

Carissa talks incessantly about the impact of this senior saint who has since "gone ahead to save her a seat in heaven." She notes, "There is a sea of Colonel Simses all around us. But there is an even bigger sea of wounded, broken, and lost young people who are hungry for time, love, and knowledge [from a mature believer]. Many of them don't know whom to ask or even what to ask. They may not come and knock on your door, but they are out there wishing they had someone to listen to them and someone who acted like they truly cared!"

I've heard it said that teenagers will listen to someone with gray hair when they *won't* listen to someone who dyes her hair—in other words, they don't want to listen to a parent or parental figure, but they are open to a grandparent's or surrogate grandparent's influence.

Carissa is now a high school senior who devotes every spare moment to her own nonprofit organization that inspires and empowers young people to "reach out along the way." She says, "It's my passion to encourage my peers to dream big and fulfill their destinies. I believe that Just REACH Ministries will mentor, educate, and develop

If you'd like to network with people in your season of life (single, retired, teen, and so on), please visit www.donnapartow.com/lylc_community to join forces with others who want to let their lives count. Stay tuned for special outreach events!

leaders of the rising generation. Given a chance, and a little support and encouragement, we will be known for how big we can dream, not for our rebellion."

Carissa operates an informative Web site, www.justreachministries .org, that keeps teens apprised of various opportunities to let their lives count, including donating teddy bears to flood victims, sponsoring a child in a Third World country, participating in a local outreach, or joining a short-term mission project. She is proof positive that every season can count.

I have worked closely with this generation of young people, and it's obvious to me that they are determined to let their lives count for God. Not only that, they have the tools, the technology, and the tenacity to finish the job of worldwide evangelization in their lifetimes. As you prayerfully consider practical ways God may be calling you to let your life count, don't overlook the option of simply being someone this next generation can count upon for spiritual and logistical support as they advance the gospel.

These determined young people are living in some of our homes, in all of our neighborhoods, and attending our churches. As those in authority, not to mention as those who control the purse strings, we have the power either to hinder them or to support their advances. If we are unwilling or unable to go oversees, will we at least support the next generation as it goes? I recently had a twenty-six-year-old missionary speak at one of my conferences, and he shared how God had challenged his mother to let him go. Your kids are not your kids; they are God's kids. By the way, they're not your grandkids either. I don't care how many scrapbooks you fill, those children belong to God, not you!

The night before we hosted our first Ignite Your Faith Teen Missions Conference (more about that in next chapter), my team gathered to pray. Thirty of us stood holding hands in a giant circle. Suddenly, I heard the voice of a young woman crying out to God, praying with a passion that blew me away. It took me a few minutes to realize it was my own teenage daughter. Most of the people holding hands that evening, including the conference director, program director, and head of the prayer ministry, were recruited from the singles' Sunday-school class at my church. Rather than sitting around worrying about their next dates, they rolled up their sleeves and wore out their knees, working and praying not for a singles' conference but for a teens' conference.

One way to let every season count is to reach out to those in different seasons of life. Mothers with preschoolers can get involved with seniors; singles can reach out to teens; seniors can share their wisdom with any age group. While I acknowledge the validity of homogeneous ministry (singles reaching singles, seniors reaching seniors), let's mix it up a bit from time to time! Because it seems we all have the same choice to make: will we make excuses or will we let our lives count?

There is so much we can learn from each other if we'll maintain teachable hearts.

People in every season of life can point to legitimate reasons why they can't let their lives count. Yet certain people in those same seasons with those same reasons actively serve God. One special way to let your life count is to deliberately reach out to those in different seasons of life.

Reflect

What season of life are you in? What perfectly legitimate excuses do you hear people in that season offering for their noninvolvement? Can you think of people who are looking for opportunities instead? Compare the two. How about you? Are you making excuses or making the most of your season?

Reach

Acquaint yourself with people in every season of life who are actively letting their lives count. Take time to listen to their stories, so the next time you hear someone (including yourself!) making excuses, recount those positive examples as motivation to move forward in ministry.

Dear heavenly Father, I thank You for the season of life I am in right now, and for all the seasons I've passed through. Help me to find balance between using this season as an excuse not to serve and taking on more than is realistic for me right now. I thank You for the people in my life who are letting every season count (teenagers, college students, singles, moms, seniors I personally know). Lord, help me to be an encouragement to each one. Father, forgive me for those times I've made excuses rather than making the most of the opportunities You brought my way. Holy Spirit, open my heart to people in other seasons who might be blessed by my involvement in their lives, both people who are younger and some who are older than me. Use me, Lord. I want every season to count! Amen.

19

Maintain a Teachable Heart

> At Gibeon the LORD appeared to Solomon during the night in a dream, and God said, "Ask for whatever you want me to give you."… "Now, O LORD my God, you have made your servant king in place of my father David. But I am only a little child and do not know how to carry out my duties. Your servant is here among the people you have chosen, a great people, too numerous to count or number. So give your servant a discerning heart to govern your people and to distinguish between right and wrong."
>
> 1 KINGS 3:5, 7–9

Whatever else may be said of Solomon, he was, from first to last, teachable. When Solomon was young (possibly in his early teens), the Lord appeared to him in a dream and offered him anything he wanted. Solomon didn't ask for health, wealth, or fame; he asked for wisdom. But he didn't say, "Make me even smarter than I already am." No, he acknowledged that he was clueless and unequal to the task set before him: "But I am only a little child and do not know how to carry out my duties" (1 Kings 3:7). God loved that response so much that He gave Solomon *more* than he asked for: "Moreover, I will give you what you have not asked for—both riches and honor—so that in your lifetime you will have no equal among kings" (verse 13).

The unlimited variety of subjects that interested Solomon ranged from childrearing (see Proverbs 22:6) and marriage (see 21:9) to diet (see 23:1–3), finances (see 22:7), business management (see 22:29), strutting roosters (see 30:31), and sex (Song of Songs). How about you? What are you interested in? Are you always learning something new: from books, sermons, audiotapes, the Internet, people around you? It's unfortunate that so many adults lose their love of learning, because learning is essential for those of us who want to let our lives count.

The simplest step on the journey to remaining teachable is developing the habit of asking questions. When you ask someone, "How is everything going?" slow down long enough to hear an honest answer. Instead of asking, "How's the family?" ask, "How did Johnny's baseball tournament go?" Instead of "How's the wife?" ask, "How is your wife's sister? I remember you mentioned she was going in for chemotherapy." And wouldn't it be great if you added this question: "Is there anything I can do?" Or how about this: "My church has a support group for cancer patients and their families. Would you like me to find out more about that for you?" Having a teachable heart means learning more about the people around you—learning about both their triumphs and tragedies. (By the way, only a teachable heart would care enough to learn what kind of support programs her church offers.)

Among everyone's three favorite words are *tell me more*. If you want to let your life count, make it your mission to learn something from everyone you meet. Remember: when you are talking about what you already know, you're not learning anything new! A story is told of a woman who had dined with two famous English statesmen, Benjamin Disraeli and William Gladstone. Afterward, she was asked her impression. "When I left the dining room after sitting next to Mr. Gladstone, I thought he was the cleverest man in England. But after sitting next to Mr. Disraeli, I thought I was the cleverest woman in England."[1]

You can be certain that Mr. Gladstone learned nothing new that evening; he was too busy holding forth on subjects in which he already considered himself an expert. How do people feel after talking with you? Something to think about, anyway. You might make it a point of asking yourself after each conversation, *How much did I learn?* If the answer is *Precious little,* you might want to work on maintaining a teachable heart.

A teachable heart is willing to learn from anyone about almost anything. One day I watched across a crowded room as the wife of my former pastor, Jennifer, listened with great interest to an elderly woman. I had never been captivated by this dear woman's endless stories, so finally my curiosity got the best of me. I marched over, determined to discover what subject matter could have commanded such rapt attention.

Knitting.

I eavesdropped for a while as Jennifer kept the conversation going with beautifully timed phrases like: "Really? Is that so? How about that! I didn't know that! I had no idea!" In other words, tell me more.

Eventually, I had to walk away to repair my mascara. Tears were streaming down my face as I finally understood why Jennifer is among the most beloved, not to mention well-informed, women I've ever known. I realize questions about knitting are not among the tough questions of life, but the real question was the one that elderly woman was asking when she entered the fellowship hall that Sunday afternoon: *Does anyone care that I'm here?*

It's the same question on the mind of almost every person you'll meet today. One of the surest ways to let your life count is to answer it with a resounding yes.

My daughter, Leah, has spent countless hours asking fishermen for their fishing secrets, and they are almost always eager to oblige. She's been on this quest from the time she was three years old! When she was nearly nine, we moved to a small town with a central lake that was routinely stocked with trout to keep the locals occupied. Leah used to walk from fisherman to fisherman, studying their techniques, looking in their tackle boxes, and asking them questions. She remained determined to learn all she could, even though she still has not caught one fish!

Leah is growing older now, and her interests have changed, but she has retained her curiosity. A teachable heart wants to know not just answers to the big questions of life (more about that in a minute) but how things work, what people care about, and of course, the when, why, and how behind *everything*. If you've ever spent time around children, you know exactly what I'm talking about! Leah is still the Question Queen!

Two years ago, God gave me a vision for a teen missions' conference. When I shared it with Leah, her teachable heart leaped with enthusiasm, "Why can't we do it *this year?*" Honestly, the thought had never crossed my mind. It seemed too impractical since I have no experience in teen ministry. But Leah was determined. When the couple who initially agreed to direct the conference had to step down for personal reasons, I decided to cancel the event. But Leah asked, "Why can't we go ahead anyway? Don't you trust God to send a new director?" *Ouch!* When God did indeed send a new director, Leah attended every planning meeting, took notes, and shared from her well-prepared research that was garnered from hours of reading teen books and magazines, surfing Christian Web sites, and interviewing friends and youth pastors. Her teachable spirit drove her to create her own crash course in teen ministry!

Nearly eight hundred people attended the first-ever Ignite Your Faith Teen Missions Conference, and it was a resounding success. An estimated sixty teens answered yes to the ultimate question: will you surrender your life to become Christ's disciple? And another two hundred fifty completed information cards stating they wanted to learn more about various mission agencies and outreach opportunities.

Later that night, Leah looked at me and smiled. "Mom, when can

For more on the Ignite Your Faith Teen Conference, visit www.igniteyourfaith.net. If you would like to help sponsor a teen outreach conference in your community, please e-mail ignite@donnapartow.com.

we get started planning *next year's conference?*" In hopes that I'll grant approval to her, she's continued studying, searching, questioning—learning all she can about today's youth and how best to reach them. Perhaps more of us should adopt such a teachable heart and remain open to fresh answers to age-old questions. At a recent youth leadership conference, Greg Stier, founder of Dare 2 Share Ministries (a national youth conference ministry), said, "We are losing half of our evangelical kids—50 percent of those raised in the church walk away from the faith."[2] According to Stier, "There are philosophy professors on every college campus who've been eating Christian freshman for breakfast for thirty years. Our kids don't stand a chance because they've never learned to answer the hard questions they are about to be confronted with."

One of the reasons why our young people, and the world at large, do not find our faith compelling is because many Christians are so quick to spout off prepackaged, superficial answers to the deep questions of life. Solomon was not afraid of the hard questions, and we shouldn't be either. Most scholars believe that he wrote the book of Ecclesiastes at the end of his life. In it, he reflects upon all that he had learned, much of it the hard way.

Not only is Ecclesiastes filled with questions, it even begins with one: "What does man gain from all his labor at which he toils under the sun?" (Ecclesiastes 1:3). Solomon poses question after question, searching honestly for answers to questions that many of us are unwilling to admit we even struggle with. But Solomon, a lifelong learner, asked, "What then do I gain by being wise?" (2:15).

People in the real world ask this kind of question every day. Students ask teachers, "Why do I need this stuff?" Employees want to know, "What does the worker gain from his toil?" (Ecclesiastes 3:9). Is the answer really a big screen television, a DVD player, a bigger house in the suburbs? Why are we doing this? Why are we working so hard? We're all going to end up dead anyway.

The other person who wasn't afraid to ask tough questions was Job. The first time he speaks, he asks: "Why did I not perish at birth, and die as I came from the womb?" (Job 3:11). In other words, he's asking God, "If You knew my life was going to be this painful, why let me be born in the first place?"

Recently, a close friend of mine lost her nephew in the Iraq War. The entire family is grappling with questions that have no easy answers. Every time I see her, I'm at loss for words. And maybe that's for the best. Sometimes the only way to let our lives count is to resist the temptation to be like Job's so-called friends, who were only too eager to serve up half-baked answers that *sounded* like wisdom but weren't truth.

Honestly, I don't know why that brave young man had to die in a war his family isn't entirely sure they believe in. I only know the Bible says God is collecting up all of our tears in a bottle (see Psalm 56:8, NLT). I know that He is the God who sees, that "in all things [He] works for the good of those who love him, who have been called according to his purpose" (Romans 8:28). I don't have all the answers, but I'm willing to listen to the questions. I'm willing to walk with my friend as she tries to learn the lessons God is teaching her through this harrowing ordeal. As I've grappled for wisdom to share with her, I've had to face some hard truths that I've avoided facing.

My objective here is not to address any of life's deeper questions but merely to say that we need to keep asking them. Keep seeking wisdom. Even at the end of his life, Solomon *was still asking questions,* still searching for wisdom, still learning, even after all he'd accomplished. People came from all over the world to listen to Solomon's wisdom (and they didn't fly in on airplanes, either); yet he didn't pretend to have arrived. He openly admitted, "Even if a wise man claims he knows, he cannot really comprehend it" (Ecclesiastes 8:17).

How about you? Are you teachable? What questions are you grappling with right now? When was the last time someone asked you a hard question about life and you admitted you hadn't quite figured that one out yet? Rather than throwing out a simplistic answer like, "Oh well, God is in control," we should be willing to acknowledge the validity of the question and be honest enough to admit some questions will never be answered this side of heaven.

What I love about Ecclesiastes is that it's not *smug*—too many of us (especially Western Christians) are smug. We think we have all the answers, but only because we live such comfortable lives. I wonder if we would be so certain of our pet theologies if we lived in the Congo or Indonesia or the West Bank? It's a question we need to be asking.

Solomon was right when he said there's a time for everything (see Ecclesiastes 3:1). And if we want to let our lives count, then it's time for God's people to start giving authentic answers to the tough questions people ask. To do so will require each of us to become and remain teachable. It will mean sitting at Jesus's feet, being lowly and humble in heart. The next time someone poses a life question, offer to get together to search the Bible or propose reading a book together. Rather than giving an answer off the top of your head, set a specific time to have a serious discussion. At the very least, follow up by giving her a book related to the topic she's inquired about.

One question on the hearts of many people is, "What happens if I make a real mess of my life?" The encouraging answer is this: even when you fall, God can still use you.

Remember

People in the real world are asking tough questions. If we want to let our lives count, we need to become lifelong learners, admitting that we don't have all the answers but that we are willing to search God's Word for wisdom.

Reflect

Are you a lifelong learner? When's the last time you had a conversation with a nonbeliever, allowing that person to challenge your beliefs? When's the last time you admitted you didn't know the answer to a question? Did you let that realization drive you to search for answers? Do you ask questions during conversations? Or do you tend to talk about what you already know?

Reach

Strike up a conversation with a total stranger in which you pose the very questions you grapple with. Have an honest dialogue, being willing to admit that although you are a Christian, you have questions that won't be answered this side of heaven. Make it a point to discover other people's worldviews! Also be willing to ask questions on topics you might consider mundane and to show sincere interest in whatever interests others.

Dear heavenly Father, I thank You for the example of men like Solomon and Job, who weren't afraid to grapple with the tough questions of life. Help me to seek You earnestly and not be content with superficial answers to deep questions. Make me sensitive to those around me who are in emotional pain, confused about why their lives are filled with suffering. Forgive me for the many conversations I've had where I've walked away having learned nothing new! Holy Spirit, teach me to be teachable! Prompt me to ask questions and show a sincere interest in the people who cross my path today. And as I show concern for their concerns, let my life count by reassuring them that at least one person cares enough to truly listen. Amen.

20

Even When You Fall, God Can Still Use You

[God] tends his flock like a shepherd:
   He gathers the lambs in his arms
and carries them close to his heart;
   he gently leads those that have young.

ISAIAH 40:11

Stan is a big, gruff outdoorsman and champion fisherman. He's the ultimate tough guy. Trust me, you wouldn't want to tangle with this dude. But he's also a father. When I see him with his daughter, Melissa, I see a different side of him. He's absolutely adorable. It was so cute to watch as he held his little baby girl in his huge, callused hands, with grease and grime under his fingernails. Anyone who saw them together could plainly see that his baby girl had stolen his heart.

When Melissa was just two years old, Stan took her to the beach. It was a magical day of sea and sunshine until tragedy struck. Some reckless persons had unlawfully brought along their own barbecue grill. Then to conceal their illegal activity, they had dumped the hot coals onto the beach, covered them up with a shallow layer of sand, and then walked away.

As Melissa went traipsing through the sand, her tiny feet landed in the bed of hot coals. She then fell into the coals, screaming out in anguish as she sustained third-degree burns over her legs and buttocks. Stan ran to his precious daughter and scooped her up in his arms to rescue her from further harm. Can you imagine his urgency as he rushed her to the nearest hospital or the hours he spent by her bedside, tenderly reassuring her that somehow, someday, she would feel okay again?

I tell this story because it offers us an incredibly accurate picture of how God cares for us. Every day, reckless people make decisions that hurt other people. But God is with us, picking us up, and bringing us to a place where we can receive comfort and healing. Few things touch the world more profoundly than the sight of a father comforting his child, whether it's an earthly father or our heavenly Father.

My favorite chapter in the Bible, Isaiah 40, recounts all of God's amazing accomplishments and attributes. Hidden in the midst of this crescendo of glory, this proclamation of God's greatness, is an interesting tidbit that reveals that our all-powerful God has a tender heart (verse 11). God is a compassionate shepherd. But not only that—He has a father's heart.

We see this side of God demonstrated in His relationship with His Son. In Jesus's hour of greatest need in the Garden of Gethsemane, He didn't proclaim the mighty attributes of Father God. Instead, "he fell to the ground and prayed that if possible the hour might pass from him. 'Abba, Father,' he said" (Mark 14:35–36). That Jesus fell to the ground and cried out the Aramaic equivalent of "Daddy" tells us what our hearts most want to know: we have a compassionate heavenly Father.

God demonstrates this characteristic most clearly when we fall. And we can let our lives count if we allow the world to watch as the God of the universe reaches down to pick us up. In Romans 8:14–15, we see: "Those who are led by the Spirit of God are sons of God. For you did not receive a spirit that makes you a slave again to fear, but you received the Spirit of sonship. And by him we cry, 'Abba.' " We cry, "Da-da." We cry, "Daddy."

My friend Martha had tried to witness to her family for nearly two decades, but they turned a deaf ear to her compelling case for Christ. She always put her best foot forward around her family so that they could see what a difference God had made in her life. She worked hard to create the perfect family, to be a role model in the church and community. She taught Sunday school and took her children to Awana. Her husband led worship with the worship team. Yet all her attempts to prove that following God had transformed her life were met with cynicism.

Then she discovered that her husband was having an affair (as her family had long suspected and accused him of), and her carefully crafted suburban-American Christian existence came crashing down. After three months of counseling, Martha opted to stop fighting to preserve a marriage she now realized was destructive on many levels. Her husband filed for divorce, and yet her church blamed her for not trying harder to hold things together.

Martha fell to the ground and cried out to her heavenly Father. She was open with her family about the devastation and disillusionment. She shared with them her doubts and fears. She dropped the Christian facade. As she stripped off the superficial trappings, her family began to notice how real God was in her life. Martha didn't just have a strict religious code to live by; she had a compassionate Father. When God prompted a Christian to send her a CD containing the song that said exactly what she needed to hear just to survive another agonizing day, she invited family members to sit and listen to it with her. When she cried on the phone to a family member on Monday, posing questions that were hard to answer, and God answered her questions through a devotional she read on Tuesday morning, she shared that too. Her family saw for themselves how God demonstrated personal care for Martha, time after time. They watched as He picked her up every time life knocked her down.

About a year after the divorce, Martha received a note from her father, thanking her for the impact she had had on his spiritual life. How? By putting on a really good show? No, simply by allowing her family to watch God work in her life in a genuine way. Eventually, Martha's father prayed to acknowledge his own need of God's compassion.

As Martha's story illustrates, even when we fall, God can still use us if we let Him. No matter what mistakes you've made in the past, your life can count. Don't be afraid to come out from the shadows or the church pew. One of the most powerful ways to let our lives count is to allow others to see God's compassion and forgiveness toward us. Of course, that will mean letting them know we've fallen.

Singer-songwriter Jamie Owens Collins once told me about a picture God gave her of heaven. As she read chapter 4 of the book of Revelation, which describes a host of angels gathered around the throne of God, she saw a group of ragtag children come barging into the throne room. God brushed aside the heavenly creatures as He stood up and reached for the children who had come seeking His help. What a beautiful illustration of what it means that we can "approach the throne of grace with confidence, so that we may receive mercy and find grace to help us in our time of need" (Hebrews 4:16).

I'm one of those Christians who tends to blow it a lot. Often when I'm hurting after a fall, I imagine myself in the midst of a throng of people who are clamoring for God's attention. I am crying out, "Daddy, Daddy, it's me!" I can't see my heavenly Father, but I know He is there, seated on His throne. Just when I feel like He could not possibly have time for me or when it feels like my latest injury is no big deal compared to what others are suffering, I'll sense the glance of God upon me. And I know my pain matters because I matter to God.

I'm blown away by the realization that any one of us, as God's children, can barge in and tell Him we've skinned our knee. We can show Him our latest boo-boo—our husband hurt our feelings, we didn't get that promotion at work, people at church are gossiping about us, whatever—and God will take time to kiss the boo-boo and begin the healing process. The angels must look upon the scene and wonder, *What's up with that?* They stand amazed because, out of everything God created in this vast universe, we have stolen His heart.

To me, that's a powerful and comforting picture. So why are we so reluctant to let the world know that God has kissed our boo-boos?

As Christians, we should be the most open and honest about our failures and falls, because that's when God shows His compassion most clearly. One of the fundamental truths in the universe is the one we sang about as children: *ashes, ashes, we all fall down.* As the Bible puts it, "All have sinned and fall short of the glory of God" (Romans 3:23). We'll never be able to signify God's perfection, but if we live transparent, authentic lives, we can accurately reflect God's compassion to a world that's desperately in need of it.

Take divorce as an example. This is an incredibly difficult subject for the church, and as a result, many Christians prefer not to talk about it if they have been divorced. The Bible clearly states that God hates divorce (see Malachi 2:16), and having seen its devastation, I understand why. We should all hate divorce. But we shouldn't hate divorced people. We should love, comfort, and care for them in practical ways. Churches can offer recovery programs such as Divorce-

If you enjoyed this chapter, you will also enjoy listening to "Knowing God," available free online. Visit www.donna partow.com and click Audios. You might also be interested in The Mighty Mavens, a ministry for women forty and up who've made their share of mistakes but who've also discovered that God gives second chances. The Mighty Mavens is for women who firmly believe that no matter what the past holds, the best is yet to come! Please visit www.mighty mavens.com.

Care[1] and provide job training (or at least teach job-hunting skills) for women who suddenly find themselves thrust into the workplace. As individuals, we can help with childcare for single parents or simply include divorced people in our social circles rather than ostracizing them.

If you have been through a divorce or a similar life trauma, be open about how God has worked in your life through that experience. Talk about the pain, but more important, talk about God's healing. Many Christians are embarrassed to even mention a past divorce. Denise was particularly ashamed because she had been through three divorces and had a child out of wedlock after one of them! She describes herself as "the woman at the well" (see John 4:5–26), and she struggled to fit in at her church. Then she heard about an outreach to female prisoners. The program director explained how the vast majority of women in prison are there because destructive relationships with men led them to make foolish choices. For example, maybe abusive fathers drove them to self-destructive behaviors such as a drug addiction, or boyfriends turned out to be a pimps who forced them into prostitution, or they finally lashed out in violence against abusive husbands.

As she listened to the stories of these women, Denise recognized her *own* story. True, she'd never been to prison, but she had lived through all of the same things that had landed other women there. She didn't know about life behind bars, but she knew all about destructive relationships with men. She knew instantly that God wanted her to share His compassion with women in prison.

Denise explains, "I can be totally open with these women about how many times I've blown it, about how God just keeps giving me one more chance, picking me up each time I fall. Twice a month I go with my cassette player, and we sing along with praise and worship music, then read a passage from the Bible, and I share what God has been teaching me. Mostly, we just cry and pray and hug, then cry and pray and hug some more.

"My mission is to go and tell them that what God did for me, He can and will do for them. Jesus loves us right where we are, just as we are, no matter what we've done. He not only forgives our sin, but He takes away the *guilt* of our sin. I had a hard time forgiving myself for what I had done, but when I finally grabbed hold of that truth, it set me free to become the woman God wanted me to be. The Bible says that she who has been forgiven much loveth much. That is why I go into the jails and share the transforming love of Jesus."

Denise doesn't talk about her divorces with everyone she meets; most people wouldn't understand and don't need to know. But God has shown her a group of women who take great comfort in her story. No doubt there's an area in your life where you struggle, and perhaps you've fallen time and time again. You don't need to tell everyone you meet about your every misstep. However, if you want to let your life count, ask God to show you those with whom you can—and should—be completely open. Not just for *their* sakes, but for yours as well.

As you invite others to witness how your heavenly Father has picked you up and helped you heal each time you have fallen, you'll be letting even the most painful experiences count. God not only picks you up, but He also puts you back in the race, which is why it's important to develop a marathon mentality.

Remember

No doubt there's an area in your life where you struggle, and perhaps you've even fallen. You don't need to tell everyone you meet about your every misstep. However, if you want to let your life count, ask God to show you those with whom you can—and should—be completely open. Not just for *their* sakes, but for yours as well.

Reflect

Recall a time in your life when you stumbled. Did you try to hide your pain and therefore hide God's compassion? Or were you open? What was the outcome?

Reach

Ask God to show you one person who is struggling in an area where you have personally experienced God's compassion (the loss of a child, prodigal child, marriage struggles, and so on). Pick up the phone and take a few minutes to tell that person the truth about your struggle and God's compassion. Then offer to pray for that person. Perhaps investigate organizations that reach out to such persons, and consider volunteering on a regular basis.

Dear heavenly Father, how can I ever thank You enough for picking me up each time I fall? I thank You for the many days and nights You've held and comforted me. Give me the courage to be open about the times I've fallen, and the wisdom to know whom I should be open with. I want to let my life count by letting others see what a compassionate God You are, but I don't want to burden people unnecessarily with details about my life they may not be able to handle. Holy Spirit, I'm counting on You to show me those people with whom I should share the painful falls You've helped me through. I want to show Your compassion to those who are in desperate need of it. Thank You in advance for the hearts You will open and the lives that will be changed. Amen.

21

Develop a Marathon Mentality

I have fought the good fight, I have finished the race, I have kept the faith. Now there is in store for me the crown of righteousness, which the Lord, the righteous Judge, will award to me on that day—and not only to me, but also to all who have longed for his appearing.

2 TIMOTHY 4:7–8

Back in 2001, I decided to run a 5K for my fortieth birthday. (Now you can calculate how old I am...have fun!) Anyway, me being me, I turned this pursuit into a major ordeal. Everyone who got within a mile of me heard all about it. I guess I expected people to stand in awe at the mere thought that I was going to run 3.2 miles. Sometimes when I was running, I would start humming the *Rocky* theme song. Then I'd imagine Sylvester Stallone coming up alongside me, demanding the opportunity to create a new reality television show about my courageous pursuit of such an illustrious goal. (If you are training for or have completed a 5K, you have every right to feel fabulous about that. I'm just saying I blew it way out of proportion.)

When I crossed the finish line, I decided I would never run another step as long as I lived! Then, earlier this year, I began praying each week with the woman who leads worship for my annual women's conference. One morning I sensed God saying, *You need to develop a marathon mentality.* I thought, *What a reminder of the marathon metaphor for the Christian life. The race is long. We have to be committed to finish what we've started. We've got to break free from the shortcut mentality and get a marathon mentality.* Yeah. I could work with that.

I started praying about it and weaving the concept into casual conversations. Then one day I heard this little Voice say, *I don't think you get it. I wasn't talking about a metaphor. I was talking about* you *getting up from behind your computer and actually running a marathon.*

God's instructions to me couldn't have been clearer: run a marathon. Instead, I ran to the store. Of course, when I say "ran to the store," I actually mean I drove to the store. Being an author and a bookaholic, I ran to a bookstore first. To demonstrate my sincerity, I bought two books and lay in bed at night reading about other people running marathons. It was great! Even as I cuddled up under the blankets with my soft, cushy pillow under my head, I could sense that marathon mentality dropping down upon me out of the sky. Ahhhhh…wonderful.

But then I sensed God saying, *No, Donna. Not wonderful. Reading a book is not running a race. I told you to run a race. Now if you want to read a book to* prepare *and to better* equip *yourself to run the*

race, I'm all in favor of it. Reading about how other people have run the
race and discovering how you *should run the race are both important.*
But don't tell yourself they are the same as getting out there and doing it.
They are not.

I figured I had better get serious, as God clearly wasn't kidding around. So I bought a couple cute running outfits and a great pair of running shoes. I didn't *exactly* obey God; I still wasn't *doing* what He told me to do, but I was willing to dress the part. I was willing to play the role; I was willing to look good on the outside. But God's Word says, "Do not merely listen to the word, and so deceive yourselves. Do what it says" (James 1:22). James further clarifies that a Christian who wants to let her life count will "be blessed in what [she] does" (verse 25).

Blessed in what she *does,* not just in what she reads about, thinks about, or wears. Don't get me wrong. Anyone who knows anything at all about me knows I love God's Word. It needs to be our daily bread. But eating bread is not an end in itself. We eat to provide fuel for our bodies so that we will have the strength to *do* what must be done. God's Word strengthens us *so that* we can run with perseverance the race God has marked out for us (see Hebrews 12:1).

It's not enough to read the Bible, although that's important. It's not enough to read Christian books like this one, although I'm glad you're reading my book. But I need to tell you the truth, friend to friend: there's something God wants you to actually do. Not just read or think about. Actually *do.* That's what letting your life count is about. Still I meet Christians all over North America who've never taken one single step beyond reading the book and buying the outfit. Never.

In fact, I've been to churches where *generations* of people, with very few exceptions, have never taken a step outside the church door. They read the Bible; they say they believe it. They go to the Christian bookstore and buy books about how other people have actually done what the Bible says we're supposed to do. They dress like nice church people. They look the part. *But they've never gotten to the part where they actually run the race!* They have never put feet to their faith, never actually obeyed the commands of God. As James warns, "Faith by itself, if it is not accompanied by action, is dead" (James 2:17). He adds, "Show me your faith without deeds, and I will show you my faith by what I do" (verse 18).

Unfortunately, many of us want to do the bare minimum. We want to take shortcuts. That's what our culture is all about. We buy exercise gadgets that supposedly do the exercise for us, and we consume potions that promise to help us lose pounds while we sleep. We

---

Yes, I finished the marathon. I ran 26.2 miles in the P.F. Chang's Rock 'n Roll Marathon in Phoenix on January 15, 2006. To view a photo of this exhausted but exuberant runner, visit www.donnapartow.com/marathon. That link also provides relevant information and resources in case this chapter inspired you to train for your own marathon. You can listen to the complete message, "Marathon Mentality," at www .donnapartow.com by clicking on Audios.

want shortcuts to health. We also want a shortcut to wealth. We Americans don't want to work for our money. We want it to drop into our laps out of a slot machine. Last year alone, my home state of Arizona spent $7.6 billion on gambling.[1] That's an average of $2,000 per adult. Coincidentally, $2,000 is about the average annual income in the South American country of Peru.[2] The average person in Arizona blows more on gambling—trying to find a shortcut to wealth—than the average person in Peru makes in an entire year.

Okay, back to my marathon story. As most of you have already guessed, I finally realized that God wanted me to actually *run* in a marathon, so I found a company that helps people prepare for their first marathon and signed up for their training program.[3] When I showed up for my first Saturday morning practice run, the coach, Brian Collins, announced that everyone was going to run a half marathon. I almost fell on the ground. But he tried to reassure me, "Don't worry, Donna. Since this is your first week, you can just run a 5K."

I said, "You've got to be kidding me. I can't run that far. Are you crazy?" Four years earlier I had trained for three months to run that far. Now after less than a week of training, this coach was telling me to "just" run a 5K, like it was nothing.

But the coach was undeterred. He looked at me and said, "You can do it. Don't overanalyze it. Don't think too much about it. Go out there and put one foot in front of the other until you get to the Gatorade station. Drink some Gatorade, then turn around and come back. I'll be right here waiting for you."

Well, that was about the craziest idea I had ever heard. Clearly, this guy didn't know what he was talking about. Then a vision of his Web site flashed through my mind. It said his company, 1st Marathon, had trained thousands of people. With my own eyes, I had just watched an army of people set out to run a half marathon at his say-so. Maybe this guy knew what he was talking about after all. Maybe a full-time marathon coach might know more than I did about training for a marathon.

It was a stretch.

But I decided that, for once in my life, I wasn't going to overanalyze the situation. I wasn't going to blow it all out of proportion. I was just going to put one foot in front of the other until I got to that Gatorade stand, and I was going to keep running until I saw my coach's face again. Whether I thought I was capable of running a 5K wasn't the issue. He was the coach. He said I was capable of doing it. He saw something in me that I didn't see in myself. My job was just to trust and obey. My job was to do what he told me to do and to forget about shortcuts. So I ran to the Gatorade stand and turned around. Then I kept running until I saw his face again. And you know what? It wasn't too hard for me.

God knows the race you're capable of running. He doesn't need you to tell Him what you think you're capable of. He'll tell you. He's the coach. Yet, we question, *Are You* sure *You want me to do this? Are You* sure *You know what you're doing in my life?* God's been training human beings to run the race of life for a long time. He knows what you are capable of, and it is so much more than you imagine, so much more than you've ever dared to attempt.

Several months ago I was in Chicago, which is quite famous

among runners for the spectacular scenic jogging path that runs alongside Lake Michigan. So I was genuinely looking forward to my scheduled hour-and-a-half run. (I was secretly hoping to bump into Oprah and convince her to have me on her show.) But somehow I ended up on the biking path instead, which led me up over a steel bridge with cars on one side, bikes on the other, and me in the middle. Dazed and confused, I tripped and fell down hard. In fact, my left knee still sports two prominent scars; I assume they're permanent.

As I sat there, in pain, bleeding, clutching my poor little knee, and having a pity party, I had a decision to make. My hotel was still a thirty-minute run away, so I had a perfectly legitimate excuse to quit. Bleeding and hurting and feeling sorry for myself, I could hail a taxi back to my hotel. Or I could get up, bleeding and hurting, and finish what I had started. One way or another, I was going to be in pain. But a long run isn't a long run when it's cut short; and when you're training for a marathon, it's the long runs that count. So even though I was tempted to let myself off the hook, I chose not to. I got back up and kept running; in fact, my decision to press on so energized me that I ran *faster* than I would have had I not fallen.

Maybe you are hurt and bleeding; maybe you have scars from what life has brought your way. Everyone does. We can all point to legitimate excuses to drop out or give up. That's why the Bible commands all of us to "run with perseverance the race marked out for us" (Hebrews 12:1). God knows all about the human tendency *not* to persevere; He knows all about our excuses.

If anyone had some legitimate excuses for quitting on God, the apostle Paul did. Here are some of his possible excuses:

Five times I received from the Jews the forty lashes minus one. Three times I was beaten with rods, once I was stoned, three times I was shipwrecked, I spent a night and a day in the open sea, I have been constantly on the move. I have been in danger from rivers, in danger from bandits, in danger from my own countrymen, in danger from Gentiles; in danger in the city, in danger in the country, in danger at sea; and in danger from false brothers. (2 Corinthians 11:24–26)

And we think *we* have scars! Imagine how crippled and disfigured Paul must have been. Can we even comprehend the constant pain he lived with? Nevertheless, Paul was going to be in pain whether he ran the race set before him or not. Like many of us, he had a choice to make. He could sit around, making excuses and feeling sorry for himself, or he could press on no matter what. Paul said, "I press on" (Philippians 3:14). As he reflected back on his life, Paul was able to say, "I have finished the race" (2 Timothy 4:7).

You can do anything God asks you to do if you are willing to simply do what God tells you to do. Trust and obey. It probably won't be half as hard as you think. That doesn't mean it will be easy, but someday you'll be able to say:

I have fought the good fight, I have finished the race, I have kept the faith. Now there is in store for me the crown of right-eousness, which the Lord, the righteous Judge, will award to me on that day—and not only to me, but also to all who have longed for his appearing. (2 Timothy 4:7–8)

A life that counts doesn't involve shortcuts. It takes a marathon mentality. If you want to let your life count, wake up each day and say, "I'm running this race to the finish line. Quitting isn't in my vocabulary. The race is long and hard, but it's not too long or too hard for me. I trust my Coach. He says I can do it. He says He'll never ask me to do more than He knows I can handle. So I know I'm going to make it!"

One day as the date for my marathon was approaching, I admitted to my coach that I was afraid I wasn't going to make it across the finish line. After nine months of training, I was starting to experience a variety of repetitive stress injuries, and I felt emotionally exhausted. He said, "Of course you'll finish, Donna. At some point during the race, you're going to have to walk for a little while. But the point is to get across that finish line in the end, and you will. But honestly, I think if you stop at the water stations long enough to drink some Gatorade, that will be enough to keep you going. Don't be like those crazy people who try to race by the water stops, either not drinking at all or trying to grab it on the go and pouring half of it all over themselves!"

He said the biggest mistake runners make is failing to pace themselves. In particular, they tend to start out too quickly, and then they bonk, which is a fun way of describing the not-fun experience of literally running out of fuel (or glycogen, if you want the technical term).

I realized that in typical Donna fashion, I had made completing the marathon an either/or proposition. Either I would run the whole way or I would grow weary and drop out of the race. Now I understood: I could run until I began to get weary, then walk for a while to regain my strength. Run and walk some more. Better still, I could make plans in advance to slow down long enough to get refreshed at the rest stops along the way. That's not cheating; that's not wimpy; that's *wisdom*!

When I shared my coach's admonition with my running partner, Starla, she explained what had happened to her during her first marathon and compared it to her Christian life: "I started out like a stallion coming out of the pen. I ran the first five miles way too fast, just like I had in my walk with God. I hadn't paced myself because of all the people cheering me on and the energy and stimuli. I tried to go too far too fast and ended up sapped of energy, just like when I became a new Christian. I was worried and distracted by the people passing me by. The entire race became a metaphor for my life. There was a guy jumping rope the whole 26.2 miles, but I could never catch up to him. He made it look so easy, just like the people who made living the Christian life look effortless while I struggled."

Eventually, Starla had to stop at the first-aid station and seek help from the medics. Somewhere around mile nineteen, she gave up her dream of running the perfect race and decided to enjoy herself. She stopped at a park long enough to hug her family and change into a fresh pair of shoes. She walked when she needed to and ran when she could. She said the greatest part was near the end of the race, where a huge crowd of spectators had formed along the sidelines. "Some I knew, some I didn't, but they were all cheering for me like they knew me." Then she heard a Voice say, *Finish strong. You may have started out too fast, you may have made mistakes along the way, but finish with your head held high. Your medal is waiting for you on the other side of the finish line.*

If you want to let your life count, pace yourself and take time to refuel, or you'll end up bonking. When you grow weary, give yourself permission to slow down for a while. If you need first aid, seek it out! You have people in your life who have made it their mission to help you run your race. If you have to walk from time to time, so be it. Your goal is the finish line; your goal is the medal; your goal is the Krispy Kreme doughnut with your name on it.

My coach's words reassured me; so did hearing Starla's story. However, my greatest comfort comes from knowing that God has called me to run this marathon. And since it was *His* idea in the first place, I know it's ultimately His responsibility to get me across the finish line. It's my job to train; it's my job to listen to my coach and do my best; but God is the author and the *finisher* of my faith. The One who called me is faithful. God would never set any of His children on a path to failure. He will never give you a race He isn't certain you can run, with His grace and power enabling you. He'll always challenge you and make you stretch, but you'll live to tell about it. I was impressed that my marathon coach had trained thousands, but God has trained billions! Trust Him. He's an expert.

I don't know what race God is calling you to run. I don't know if you've bonked or if you're sitting at the first-aid station while you read these words. I do know God Himself has called you to let your life count—that's why you picked up this book and why you are, even now, passing an important milestone. I encourage you to pace yourself, refuel, and refresh; walk when you need to. Please know that I'm part of the great cloud of witnesses cheering you on. Although I may not know your name, I'm praying for you—praying you'll do more than read the book, more than buy the outfit. I'm praying you'll get in the race and run it to the finish line because you have made the decision to let your life count.

Remember

There are no shortcuts to a life that counts; we must develop a marathon mentality. Reading about the Christian life is not the same as *running with perseverance* the race marked out for you.

Reflect

Do you sometimes substitute reading the book, wearing the outfit, or looking the part for actually running the race? Are you running the race God has set before you, or are you sitting on the sidelines? What is God calling you to do? Have you bonked? Do you need to stop at the first-aid station or slow down and walk for a while?

Reach

Sometimes a runner needs a good coach! We call them mentors, role models, shepherds. Do you need a coach? Pray about some possibilities, and then reach out and ask. Or could you even be a coach? Pray about some possibilities, and then reach out and offer.

Dear heavenly Father, I thank You for seeing me through to the milestone of finishing this book on letting my life count. I thank You for the many experiences I've had along the way, as the Holy Spirit has taught me to follow His leading. I'm amazed how simple, and yet how challenging, this process has been. Father, thank You for reminding me that it's okay to walk sometimes, that just because I've grown weary doesn't mean I have to permanently drop out of the race. I can rest; I can seek first aid if I need it. I'm so grateful for the people who cheer me on; help me to spur others on toward love and good deeds. Use me, not only to let my life count, but as one who inspires others to let their lives count as well. It's such a comfort to know that You've called me to run this race and that You're going to get me across that finish line. Dear Jesus, I look forward to seeing You when my race is through. Have my medal ready! Amen.

CONCLUSION

One Life Can Change History

y father once said to me, "You know, Donna. You kids think I was some great hero because I won a few medals. I wasn't a hero. I was just a teenager." Just a teenager living in a critical moment in human history. My father knew he couldn't possibly save the world from the madness that was reigning during World War II. But he also knew that he couldn't sit idly by. So he enlisted in the 101st Airborne Division, determined to do what he could. My dad explained to me that when you strapped on a parachute and jumped out of that plane, you had *no idea* where you would land or what you would find. All you knew was that there were people trapped behind enemy lines and it was your job to find them and set them free. In fact, my father was with a team of soldiers who liberated one of the concentration camps.

In the same way, God wants to drop us behind enemy lines, and when we hit the ground, all we have to do is look around for someone who needs to be rescued from the control of the Enemy, then do all we can to set them free. The fact is, if you are living on planet Earth, you *are* behind enemy lines, and you *are* surrounded by people who are being held captive. Yet "our struggle is not against flesh and blood, but against the rulers, against the authorities, against the powers of this dark world and against the spiritual forces of evil in the heavenly realms" (Ephesians 6:12).

Perhaps you, like me, are too young to remember World War II. My father and mother sure remember, and I grew up hearing their stories. Those were some of the darkest days in human history. Millions of people were being slaughtered. In the first part of the war, the outcome of this great struggle rested largely on the shoulders of Great Britain. The forces of darkness were aligning against them, ready to launch a merciless attack against their small islands. Their prime minister, Winston Churchill, took to the airwaves on June 18, 1940, and spoke to his people, saying these immortal words:

The whole fury and might of the enemy must very soon be turned on us.... If we can stand up to [Hitler], all Europe may be free and the life of the world may move forward into broad, sunlit uplands. But if we fail, then the whole world... will sink into the abyss of a new Dark Age.... Let us therefore brace ourselves to our duties, and so bear ourselves that, if the British Empire...last[s] for a thousand years, men will still say, "This was their finest hour."[1]

It's obvious in our day that the spiritual forces of darkness have aligned themselves against the nations of the earth and against the people of God. On July 7, 2005, terrorists struck London in the worst attacks that nation has experienced since the Second World War. The spiritual future of countless millions, possibly billions, of people is at stake. Will we leave them dying in darkness? Will we sit idly by, or will we let our lives count? Will we, like my father, strap on our parachutes and let God drop us behind enemy lines? Are we willing to go *wherever* He sends us—even to the darkest and most dangerous territory?

Let us brace ourselves and so bear ourselves that we finally finish the job. It is time for us as Christians to go in the power of God so that the glory of God will be revealed to the ends of the earth. Then when the gospel light of God's glory reaches into the last dark corner of the earth, the trumpet will sound, the heavens will part, and Jesus Christ will return in triumph.

He will return declaring, "Well done, good and faithful generation. At last, you have finished the assignment I gave two thousand years ago. It's time to celebrate." Someday we will stand in heaven, surrounded by that great cloud of witnesses of which Scripture speaks, as all of heaven proclaims, "Surely this was the church's finest hour." Will you be counted among those who arose in this hour to let their lives count?

I want to share something very personal. God spoke to me as I was praying several months ago. He said, *Donna, do you want to be small? It's all about you. You and your problems, you and your hurts. You right at the center of the universe. That's okay. I'll still love you; you'll still go to heaven. But that's not the way I created you to live. You can be small if you want to, but you cannot be small and be part of what I'm doing in the world.*

It was almost as if He was waiting for my answer. I knew that in that moment I was free to decide what kind of life I wanted. Did I want to let my life to count or not? It was the valley of decision for me. John Wesley said, "Some people want to live within the sound of chapel bells, but I want to run a mission a yard from the gates of hell." It's no coincidence that John Wesley changed the course of history.

Those of us who are alive today have the advantage of coming behind the many Christians who have let their lives count because they took the Great Commission seriously, and through them God's purposes were accomplished. It's amazing how much God can do through one person who is willing to let his or her life count. Maybe you've been tempted to think, *I'm only one person, what can I do?* One person in the center of God's purpose is enough to change the course of history! As a bonus encouragement to you, I'd like to give you a brief overview of how the gospel has advanced throughout history, beginning with the work of the twelve disciples.[2] Martin Luther said they so effectively spread the gospel that the Great Commission had been fulfilled and Jesus was due back on planet Earth momentarily. (In case you're not a history buff, he said that back in the 1500s.) Well, Martin Luther missed that one, but he was right that the disciples did make incredible progress.

Apparently, the twelve disciples divided up the map of the known world and headed out to get the job done. They took Jesus seriously. Andrew went to Russia, Turkey, and Greece, where it's said he was crucified. Thomas went to India, where it's believed he was speared to death. Philip went to North Africa, where he was arrested and killed. Matthew ministered in Iran and Ethiopia, where he was stabbed to death. Bartholomew went to India, Armenia, Ethiopia, and Southern Arabia, where he was killed. James ministered in Syria, where he was stoned then clubbed to death. Simon went to Iran, where he was executed for refusing to worship the sun god. Matthias, who replaced Judas, went to Syria, where he was burned to death. Peter ministered in Northern Turkey and, as most Christians know, was crucified upside down in Rome. John is the only disciple believed to have died a natural death.

While the disciples were fulfilling their assignments, the apostle Paul was doing the same by going on several missionary journeys into Asia and Europe. He was beheaded for his efforts. This handful of men risked their lives to share the gospel, and in the process they turned the Roman Empire upside down.

After this initial evangelistic thrust, the church largely ignored the Great Commission until the time of Patrick.[3] Although many people think Patrick, or Saint Patrick as he is more commonly called, is Irish, he was actually born in England about AD 389. He was kidnapped at age sixteen and sold as a slave in Ireland. It was there that he encountered God in such a powerful way that even after escaping slavery and making it safely home to England, he dared to return to Ireland and planted more than two hundred churches as the first real Christian missionary since the time of the early church.

Patrick led more than one hundred thousand people to Christ and established a vibrant church in a dark and dangerous land where Druids practiced human sacrifice. Substantial evidence of the missionary efforts of his followers can be found all over Europe, from Russia to Iceland and everywhere in between. Then the world fell into the

Dark Ages, and the gospel failed to advance into new territory for more than one thousand years. Thankfully, Patrick's followers preserved Scripture and other Christian and classical literature at their monasteries (as described in the outstanding book *How the Irish Saved Civilization* by Thomas Cahill).

Yet for more than one thousand years, the church largely neglected our assignment. There were a few exceptions, but no major push forward. Granted there were the Reformation and the Counter Reformation in Europe, but the church wasn't taking the Great Commission into new territory. They were just fighting over old turf. That's what the church always does: either we advance the Great Commission abroad or we fight with each other at home.

In the early 1700s, an extraordinary woman named Susannah Wesley not only had a vibrant ministry of her own, but she also raised more than a dozen children, including John and Charles, who had a profound spiritual impact beginning in their native land of England. The movement spread to the United States through the ministry of their friend George Whitefield, who conducted a preaching tour of the American Colonies from 1739 to 1740. Whitefield, along with Jonathan Edwards, became part of a mighty revival in America in the middle of the eighteenth century known as the Great Awakening. During this same period in history, David Brainerd[4] died while working with Native Americans in the first real cross-cultural outreach since Patrick's followers sailed to the tip of North America.

In the wake of this great revival, many of America's greatest universities, such as Princeton (1746), Brown (1764), Rutgers (1766), and Dartmouth (1769), were founded with the specific goal of preparing students for service as ministers. Unfortunately, by the early 1790s, Christians were so few on American college campuses that they met in secret and kept their minutes in code so that no one would know what they were about. A poll taken at Harvard discovered not one Christian in the whole student body. Princeton had two Christians.

But then Christians started praying in earnest.

In 1792, William Carey[5] published a book outlining the responsibilities of Christians to a lost world. Carey was the first influential person in more than one thousand years—since the time of Patrick's followers—to say, "Maybe we need to take the Great Commission seriously." That's why he's known as the Father of Modern Missions. He was the first to boldly say, "If we want to enjoy all the benefits of

If this chapter sparked your interest in Christian history, visit www.donnapartow.com/history for more resources, including information on a fascinating college-level course on the history of missions, available online or at local churches around the United States. You can also listen to a message on the advance of the gospel, "Behind Enemy Lines," by visiting www.donnapartow.com and clicking Audios. Please remember to share *your* story about how God is impacting the world through you! People are waiting to hear from you at www .donnapartow.com/lylc_community. Who knows? Your testimony might be the spark that lights the flame that changes the world!

faith as described in Scripture, shouldn't we also be willing to make the sacrifices required?"

Carey himself went as a missionary to India, but more important, he inspired tens of thousands of others to let their lives count by taking the gospel where it had never been preached. The entire modern missionary movement started with just one man with a willing heart.

Among those William Carey inspired were five young men who read his book and were meeting for prayer on the campus of Williams College in Massachusetts in 1806. When a rainstorm hit, they moved to a nearby haystack. Their informal prayer meeting launched what is called the Haystack Revival—a movement that sent more than twelve hundred missionaries to the coastlands of China, India, Africa, and the South Seas. For the first time, women were well-positioned to let their lives count—not just alongside their husbands (as women had done for centuries), but as part of a new movement of single women missionaries, including Amy Carmichael,[6] who rescued children from temple prostitution in India; Gladys Aylward, who led one hundred children on a harrowing journey to safety in war-torn China (watch the movie about her life, *The Inn of the Sixth Happiness* starring Ingrid Bergman); and Helen Roseveare,[7] a medical missionary to Africa who became an international missionary spokesperson after her retirement.

It started with five college students who were determined to let their lives count.

Between 1824 and 1837, American evangelist Charles Finney[8] led more than half a million people to Christ and fought for social reform, arguing that the gospel should change the way we live and, as a result, turn society upside down. Indeed, entire communities were transformed by the presence and power of God working through His people. It started with one man who was determined to let his life count.

In 1853, Hudson Taylor[9] sailed for China at the age of twenty-one. One of the first Chinese Christians asked him, "How long have you in the West known this good news?" Hudson Taylor was ashamed to admit the answer: nearly two thousand years. The astonished Chinese gentleman asked, "Why didn't you come sooner?" With that challenge burning in his heart, Hudson Taylor started the China Inland Mission.[10] He said it wasn't enough to reach the coastlands; every province in China had the right to hear the gospel message. By 1895, the China Inland Mission had 641 missionaries and 462 Chinese helpers at 260 mission stations.

In September 1857, Jeremiah Lanphier put an ad in the newspaper that he was starting a businessmen's prayer meeting in Manhattan. In a city of one million people, six showed up. The second week fourteen came; the next, twenty-three. The group decided to meet every day during their lunch hour for prayer. Within six months, ten thousand people were gathering daily for prayer in New York City. Each week, ten thousand people were becoming Christians in New York City alone.

When the revival reached Chicago, a young shoe salesman asked if he could teach Sunday school at his church. He was turned down, so he began teaching kids he found on the streets. That young man's name was D. L. Moody.[11] In Chicago, largely through the influence of this one man, more than a million people came to God in one year. Then that same revival jumped the Atlantic Ocean, traveling to Scotland and Wales, then England, parts of Europe, South Africa, and India. Its effects were felt for forty years. It began with one shoe salesman whose offer to teach Sunday school was declined. Guess they didn't think he would count for much. But actually, it began with one man putting one ad in a newspaper that attracted the interest of six people. Doesn't seem like that would count for much, either. But God can accomplish extraordinary things through the lives of ordinary people with willing hearts.

In 1904, a great revival began in Wales[12] with a twenty-six-year-old coal miner turned seminary student named Evan Roberts, who asked his pastor if he could teach. The pastor said, "Well, not on Sunday you can't! But if you want to say a few words at the Monday night prayer meeting that no one attends, go for it." (Okay, I'm paraphrasing!) Then the pastor didn't even let him speak *at* the prayer meeting. Instead, he announced, "Our young brother feels he has a message for you if you care to wait to hear him after tonight's prayer meeting." I guess he didn't think he could count on Evan!

Seventeen people stayed, and revival began that night. It's said that the revival swept like a tidal wave over Wales. In five months, one hundred thousand people came to Christ. The social impact was astounding. Judges had no cases to try: there was literally no crime. From that tiny country, with one young man, revival swept Britain, Scandinavia, Germany, North America, Australia, Africa, Brazil, Mexico, and Chile. It began with one person, just as it always does.

In 1934, Cameron Townsend caught the vision for Bible translation after a Guatamalan asked him, in essence, "If God's so smart, why doesn't He speak my language?" Great question! Since then, Wycliffe

Bible Translators[13] has provided Bibles in 623 languages around the world and helped spark an interest in minority group languages. They are currently working on 1,294 languages with at least 3,700 languages still needing God's Word. Wycliffe urgently needs more than seven thousand new missionaries if they are going to achieve their goal of beginning programs for every language group needing God's Word by 2025. This vision for reaching the world all began with one man who was willing to let his life count. One such person is all God needs.

I believe another great wave of revival is about to be released upon the earth. I believe a spiritual tsunami is about to hit this planet such as the world has never known. And because every great move of God began somewhere with someone, I ask you: why can't it begin with you? Stop believing that your life couldn't possibly count in such a powerful way. It can!

A tsunami starts with underwater earthquakes. You can't see them; you don't even feel them; you don't even know they're happening. Such spiritual earthquakes are happening in nations around the world in places such as Uganda, Colombia, and China.

In July 2005, I had the privilege of traveling to Panama with Focus on the Family's *Brio* magazine staff and approximately five hundred short-term missionaries.[14] Focus on the Family representatives made arrangements to perform their musical drama *Spellbound* in public schools around the country. Each day more than a dozen teams of thirty went into elementary and high schools, often doing three to five performances a day. As a result of this ten-day outreach, an estimated eighteen thousand Panamanians prayed to ask Christ into their lives. That's just one story of one trip made by one Christian organization into one small country on this vast globe. God is moving!

The opportunities for *you* to let your life count on short-term (or even long-term) mission trips are numerous and truly unprecedented. We are living during a tremendously exciting time in church history. In previous centuries, it took missionaries *months* to arrive at their destinations. It's a brand-new day, and every person reading this book is no more than a long flight away from the front line of the gospel's advance. Truly, we are the most blessed people in history.

What will it take to finally finish the assignment Jesus gave to His disciples more than two thousand years ago? It will take what it has always taken: one person. One person whose determination to live a life that counts *inspires* a generation.

Are you that person?

SEVEN STEPS TO FREEDOM

1. Know that God loves you.

"For God so loved the world that he gave his one and only Son, that whoever believes in him shall not perish but have eternal life" (John 3:16).

2. Acknowledge your sin.

"For all have sinned and fall short of the glory of God" (Romans 3:23).

"If we confess our sins, he is faithful and just and will forgive us our sins and purify us from all righteousness" (1 John 1:9).

3. Turn from sin.

"Therefore do not let sin reign in your mortal body so that you obey its evil desires. Do not offer the parts of your body to sin, as instruments of wickedness, but rather offer yourselves to God" (Romans 6:12–13).

4. Accept that Jesus is the only way.

"I am the way and the truth and the life. No one comes to the Father except through me" (John 14:6).

"Salvation is found in no one else, for there is no other name under heaven given to men by which we must be saved" (Acts 4:12).

5. Realize that Jesus paid the penalty for your sins.

"But he was pierced for our transgressions, he was crushed for our iniquities; the punishment that brought us peace was upon him, and by his wounds we are healed. We all, like sheep, have gone astray, each of us has turned to his own way; and the LORD has laid on him the iniquity of us all" (Isaiah 53:5–6).

6. Receive Jesus as your Savior.

"If you confess with your mouth, 'Jesus is Lord,' and believe in your heart that God raised him from the dead, you will be saved. For it is with your heart that you believe and are justified, and it is with your mouth that you confess and are saved.... For 'Everyone who calls on the name of the Lord will be saved'" (Romans 10:9–10, 13).

"Here I am! I stand at the door and knock. If anyone hears my voice and opens the door, I will come in and eat with him, and he with me" (Revelation 3:20).

7. Follow God daily as part of His family.

"Yet to all who received him, to those who believed in his name, he gave the right to become children of God" (John 1:12).

NOTES

Chapter 1

1. The date was 29 August 2005.
2. I regret that I do not have any further details. I heard this on Christian radio.

Chapter 2

1. A longer version of this story originally appeared on my Web site and is adapted here by permission of the author.
2. If you'd like to learn more about the Button Brigade, a ministry that distributes a line of button jewelry and donates the proceeds to AIDS orphans, visit www.donnapartow.com/buttons.

Chapter 3

1. *American Dictionary of the English Language,* Noah Webster 1828 edition. San Francisco, CA: Foundation for American Christian Education.
2. *American Dictionary of the English Language.*
3. An e-mail received by the author.

Chapter 4

1. *The Works of John Wesley* (1872 edition by Thomas Jackson), vol. 11, no. 29, 366–446; Wesley Center Online, http://wesley.nnu.edu.

2. Presentation by Dee Duke, 10 June 2004, at PrayerQuake 2004 in Mesa, AZ.

3. Corrie ten Boom, *Marching Orders for the End Battle* (London: Christian Literature Crusade, 1970).

4. E. M. Bounds, *E. M. Bounds on Prayer* (New Kensington, PA: Whitaker, 1997), 11–12, 22.

5. Charles Spurgeon, quoted in Bounds, *On Prayer,* 44.

6. Bounds, *On Prayer,* 69.

Chapter 5

1. Brother Lawrence, *The Practice of the Presence of God* (New Kensington, PA: Whitaker, 1982), 8.

2. The Bible indicates that the presence of the Lord has a profound impact, not just on individuals (the wicked perish, Psalm 68:2), but on cities (they are broken down, Zephaniah 3:6), nations (which tremble, Habakkuk 3:6) and even the physical world (trees shout for joy, 1 Chronicles 16:33, and the earth quakes and trembles, Nahum 1:5 and Psalm 114:7).

3. Author' notes taken during Jackson Senyonga's sermon at PrayerQuake, 10 June 2004, Mesa, AZ.

4. Author's notes, Jackson Senyonga's sermon.

Chapter 6

1. Ravi Zacharias, address to the United Nations' Prayer Breakfast, 10 September 2002, www.rzim.org/publications/essay_arttext.php?id=13.

2. That's 70,000 million, million, million or
   70,000,000,000,000,000,000,000. Robert Roy Britt,
   "Imperfect Estimate Claims Universe Has 70 Sextillion
   Stars," 22 July 2003, www.space.com/scienceastronomy/
   star_count_030722.html.
3. Adapted from the "Passport Challenge" booklet developed by
   Word of Grace Church. Used by permission.
4. This statistic is taken from the Services section of www.salvation
   army.org.
5. This statistic is taken from www.nigeriafirst.org/article_3939
   .shtml.

Chapter 7

1. Rick Rusaw and Eric Swanson, *The Externally Focused
   Church* (Loveland, CO: Group, 2004), 112.

Chapter 10

1. Andrew Murray, *Humility* (Minneapolis: Bethany,
   2001), 53.

Chapter 11

1. If you have not read any of my previous works and are
   interested in my testimony, I would suggest *This Isn't the
   Life I Signed Up For* (Minneapolis: Bethany, 2003).
2. For more information on Adopt-A-Block, visit the
   Outreach/Ministries section of www.dreamcenter.org.

3. For more information, visit www.freewheelchair
mission.org.

Chapter 16

1. Author's notes, Jackson Senyonga's sermon.
2. "Area Intel on Turkey," Operation Reveille, www.oprev.org/
TurkeyIntel.htm.

Chapter 19

1. This quotation is taken from www.leadershipnow.com/
charismaquotes.html.
2. Greg Stier presentation, 11 October 2005, in Phoenix, AZ.

Chapter 20

1. For more information, visit www.divorcecare.com.

Chapter 21

1. This statistic is taken from www.aznews.us/arizona_indian_
casinos_hit_big_jackpot.htm.
2. This statistic is taken from www.worldbank.org under the
Eligibility Borrowing section.
3. For more information, visit www.1stmarathon.com.

Conclusion

1. Winston Churchill, "Their Finest Hour" speech to the
House of Commons, 18 June 1940, www.winston
churchill.org/i4a/pages/index.cfm?pageid=418.

2. For a fascinating and inspiring look at the history of missions, consider taking the thirteen-week Worldwide Perspectives Course. Visit www.worldwideperspectives.org for details. Please see also http://chi.gospelcom.net.

3. You can read a beautiful devotional incorporating the history and writings of Patrick and his followers entitled *Celtic Daily Prayer.*

4. Many Christians, including martyred missionary Jim Elliot, have been profoundly influenced by David Brainerd's journals, which were published after his death. Read *The Life and Diary of David Brainerd* by Philip E. Howard Jr.

5. Christian History Institute has produced a DVD on the life of William Carey, *Candle in the Dark.*

6. Elisabeth Elliot has written a tremendous biography of Amy Carmichael entitled *A Chance to Die.*

7. Helen Rosevear's autobiography is one of the most life-changing books I've ever read. Although currently out of print, *Give Me This Mountain* can be tracked down via the Internet.

8. Bethany House has updated and reprinted much of Charles Finney's writings, including two of my favorite books, *Principles of Prayer* and *Answers to Prayer.*

9. Hudson Taylor's son and daughter-in-law, Howard and Mary Taylor, wrote an influential book about his life and ministry entitled *Hudson Taylor's Spiritual Secret.*

10. This mission agency still operates today and is now known as Overseas Missionary Fellowship. For details, visit www .omf.org.

11. For more on his life and ministry, read *The D. L. Moody Collection: The Highlights of His Writings, Sermons, Anecdotes, and Life Story,* edited by James S. Bell Jr.

12. Many Christians are fascinated by the Welsh Revival, and there are numerous Web sites devoted to the topic, including www.welshrevival.com.

13. For more on the ongoing ministry of Wycliffe Bible Translators, visit www.wycliffe.org.

14. For more information on *Brio* magazine's annual mission trip for teenagers, visit www.briomag.com/missions. I highly recommend it.

ABOUT THE AUTHOR

*B*est-selling author and Christian communicator DONNA PARTOW travels worldwide, sharing her testimony of God's transforming power and challenging her audience's preconceived notions about what it takes to let our lives count.

Her previous books, including *Becoming a Vessel God Can Use,* *This Isn't the Life I Signed Up For,* and *Becoming the Woman I Want to Be,* have sold more than three quarters of a million copies worldwide and have been translated into numerous languages.

Donna toured with the Women of Virtue conference team for several years and currently partners with Focus on the Family, Wycliffe, and other ministries to promote outreach as a lifestyle. If your church or organization would like to host a Let Your Life Count conference for adults and teens, please e-mail lylc@donnapartow.com or visit www.donnapartow.com.

The Key Point and Scripture Cards on the following pages are designed for you to cut out and use as a guide to let your life count. Put them where you can easily refer to them, such as in your pocket, wallet, purse, or planner, or on your message board or the mirror in your bathroom—wherever is convenient to you.

Keep these cards as a reminder of what God wants to do through you. Remember, when who you are and how you live reflect God's heart, your life will truly count for eternity.

1
YOUR LIFE CAN COUNT

2
JUST BE YOURSELF

"Then the righteous will answer him, 'Lord, when did we see you hungry and feed you, or thirsty and give you something to drink? When did we see you a stranger and invite you in, or needing clothes and clothe you? When did we see you sick or in prison and go to visit you?' The King will reply, 'I tell you the truth, whatever you did for one of the least of these brothers of mine, you did for me'" (Matthew 25:37–40).

Your life can and will count—in small ways and large, in ways you might expect and in ways beyond your imagination—if you'll simply open your eyes to the world around you and open your heart to the possibility that you might be someone's answer to prayer.

"For by the grace given me I say to every one of you: Do not think of yourself more highly than you ought, but rather think of yourself with sober judgment, in accordance with the measure of faith God has given you. Just as each of us has one body with many members, and these members do not all have the same function, so in Christ we who are many form one body, and each member belongs to all the others. We have different gifts, according to the grace given us" (Romans 12:3–6).

God created you to be you and placed you on this earth with your skills, interests, and life experiences at this precise moment in time for a reason; don't thwart His plan. Be yourself.

3
DON'T TRY TO MAKE
YOUR LIFE COUNT

4
DISCOVER
GOD-DIRECTED PRAYER

"Being confident of this, that he who began a good work in you will carry it on to completion until the day of Christ Jesus" (Philippians 1:6).

The potential pitfall for those of us who want to let our lives count comes when we shift gears from simply *letting* to frantically trying to *make* our lives count. Your life can count when you forget trying to make something happen and simply let your life be available to God.

"This is the confidence we have in approaching God: that if we ask anything according to his will, he hears us. And if we know that he hears us—whatever we ask—we know that we have what we asked of him" (1 John 5:14–15).

Effective prayer consists not in telling God what to do but in listening as He tells us what He wants to do. One of the reasons many prayers go unanswered is that our prayer lists are too much like shopping lists. We fail to realize that God has the real prayer list. Let God direct your prayer time!

5
LIVE DAILY
IN GOD'S PRESENCE

6
YOU WERE CREATED TO BE
A SIGN THAT GOD CARES

"Then Moses said to him, 'If your Presence does not go with us, do not send us up from here'" (Exodus 33:15).

In the presence of God, the possibility for miracles always exists. We can walk in the presence and power of God even as we go about our daily routines.

"He comes alongside us when we go through hard times, and before you know it, he brings us alongside someone else who is going through hard times so that we can be there for that person just as God was there for us" (2 Corinthians 1:4, MSG).

You were created to be a sign to the world that God is real and that He cares. Open your heart to the possibility that you might be the answer to someone's prayer: "God, if You care, show me a sign."

7
GOD HAS PREPARED GOOD WORKS FOR YOU TO DO

8
YOU DON'T HAVE TO BE A CHURCH INSIDER TO COUNT

"For it is by grace you have been saved, through faith—and this not from yourselves, it is the gift of God—not by works, so that no one can boast. For we are God's workmanship, created in Christ Jesus to do good works, which God prepared in advance for us to do" (Ephesians 2:8–10).

God has assignments and divine appointments prepared for each of us every day. There is no prepackaged formula that we can all follow, because God has prepared works that are specifically suited to who you are and the life you live.

"Then the King will say to those on his right, 'Come, you who are blessed by my Father; take your inheritance, the kingdom prepared for you since the creation of the world. For I was hungry and you gave me something to eat, I was thirsty and you gave me something to drink, I was a stranger and you invited me in, I needed clothes and you clothed me, I was sick and you looked after me, I was in prison and you came to visit me.'...

"The King will reply, 'I tell you the truth, whatever you did for one of the least of these brothers of mine, you did for me.'" (Matthew 25:34–36, 40).

You don't have to be a church insider to let your life count. Many people outside the church walls need to see the love of God.

9
DON'T WAIT UNTIL
YOU FEEL GOOD ENOUGH

10
WALK IN HUMILITY

"Not that I have already obtained all this, or have already been made perfect, but I press on to take hold of that for which Christ Jesus took hold of me" (Philippians 3:12).

Very few people ever feel good enough to serve God, and those who do are self-deceived. Even the apostle Paul acknowledged that he hadn't arrived spiritually, but he was pressing on. We should do likewise.

"Humble yourselves [feeling very insignificant] in the presence of the Lord, and He will exalt you [He will lift you up and make your lives significant]" (James 4:10, AMP).

Pride is a very real potential pitfall for those who want to let their lives count, and that's why it's important to cultivate humility. But humility doesn't mean thinking less of yourself, it means thinking of yourself less.

11
LET CHRIST'S LOVE
COMPEL YOU

12
PRESS THROUGH
HINDRANCES

"If you love me, you will obey what I command" (John 14:15).

It's possible to obey God for the wrong reasons. Duty-driven or formula-driven Christianity leads to burnout or disillusionment. Only love-compelled obedience will enable us to let our lives count.

"Therefore, since we are surrounded by such a great cloud of witnesses, let us throw off everything that hinders and the sin that so easily entangles, and let us run with perseverance the race marked out for us" (Hebrews 12:1).

If you want to let your life count, you will have to press through hindrances. Fortunately, God can help you overcome those hindrances, bringing greater glory to Himself. Don't be surprised when they come. Be determined to throw them off.

13
DARE TO DO
THE THING YOU DREAD

14
DO IT AFRAID

"For God did not give us a spirit of timidity, but a spirit of power, of love and of self-discipline. So do not be ashamed to testify about our Lord" (2 Timothy 1:7–8).

Dread, which is a form of fear, is not from God. Dread causes us to procrastinate and avoid doing those things we should be doing in order to let our lives count. So dare to do the thing you dread.

"To keep me from becoming conceited because of these sur-passingly great revelations, there was given me a thorn in my flesh, a messenger of Satan, to torment me. Three times I pleaded with the Lord to take it away from me. But he said to me, 'My grace is sufficient for you, for my power is made per-fect in weakness.' Therefore I will boast all the more gladly about my weaknesses, so that Christ's power may rest on me" (2 Corinthians 12:7–9).

Everyone has fears and personal insecurities. Don't use your personal insecurities as a license to disobey God. Instead, make the decision to "do it afraid."

15
EVEN YOUR PROBLEMS CAN COUNT

16
BE WILLING TO SACRIFICE

"Dear friends, do not be surprised at the painful trial you are suffering, as though something strange were happening to you. But rejoice that you participate in the sufferings of Christ, so that you may be overjoyed when his glory is revealed" (1 Peter 4:12–13).

Everyone has problems, not just you! Far from disqualifying you for kingdom service, your problems—if handled correctly—will be the very things that will enable you to let your life count.

"Therefore, I urge you, brothers, in view of God's mercy, to offer your bodies as living sacrifices, holy and pleasing to God—this is your spiritual act of worship" (Romans 12:1).

As Christians, we are called to offer spiritual sacrifices, even offering ourselves as living sacrifices. There is no easy way to become the person God has called you to be, no easy way to do what God has called you to do, no other way to let your life count.

17
Overshadowed Doesn't Mean Overlooked

18
Let Every Season Count

"Your Father, who sees what is done in secret, will reward you" (Matthew 6:18).

Being overshadowed doesn't mean being overlooked. It's not always the person who gets the most attention whose life counts most. Those things you do for His kingdom, even if they are overshadowed now, will be rewarded openly in eternity.

"There is a time for everything, and a season for every activity under heaven" (Ecclesiastes 3:1).

Everyone in every season of life can point to legitimate reasons why they can't let their lives count. Yet people in those same seasons with those same reasons actively serve God. One very special way to let your life count is to deliberately reach out to those in a different season of life.

19
Maintain
a Teachable Heart

20
Even When You Fall,
God Can Still Use You

"At Gibeon the LORD appeared to Solomon during the night in a dream, and God said, 'Ask for whatever you want me to give you.'...

"'Now, O LORD my God, you have made your servant king in place of my father David. But I am only a little child and do not know how to carry out my duties. Your servant is here among the people you have chosen, a great people, too numerous to count or number. So give your servant a discerning heart to govern your people and to distinguish between right and wrong'" (1 Kings 3:5, 7–9).

People in the real world are asking tough questions. If we want to let our lives count, we need to become lifelong learners, admitting that we don't have all the answers, but are willing to search God's Word for wisdom.

"[God] tends his flock like a shepherd: He gathers the lambs in his arms and carries them close to his heart; he gently leads those that have young" (Isaiah 40:11).

No doubt there's an area in your life where you struggle, and perhaps you've even fallen. You don't need to tell everyone you meet about your every misstep. However, if you want to let your life count, ask God to show you those with whom you can and should be completely open. Not just for their sakes, but for yours as well.

21
DEVELOP A
MARATHON MENTALITY

"I have fought the good fight, I have finished the race, I have kept the faith. Now there is in store for me the crown of righteousness, which the Lord, the righteous Judge, will award to me on that day—and not only to me, but also to all who have longed for his appearing" (2 Timothy 4:7–8).

There are no shortcuts to a life that counts; we must develop a marathon mentality. Reading about the Christian life is not the same as running with perseverance the race marked out for you.